IT HAPPENED
IN INDIA

Prithvi Kandarker
Bought from 'Big Bazar'
Bangalore - July 2007

IT HAPPENED
IN INDIA

The story of Pantaloons, Big Bazaar,
Central and the great Indian consumer

KISHORE BIYANI
WITH DIPAYAN BAISHYA

Rupa & Co

Published 2007 by
Rupa & Co
7/16, Ansari Road, Daryaganj,
New Delhi 110 002
Sales Centres:
Allahabad Bangalooru Chandigarh Chennai
Hyderabad Jaipur Kathmandu
Kolkata Mumbai Pune

Typeset in Weiss BT by
Nikita Overseas Pvt. Ltd.
1410 Chiranjiv Tower
43 Nehru Place
New Delhi 110 019

Printed in India by
Gopsons Papers Ltd.
A-14 Sector 60
Noida 201 301

*This book is dedicated to all the
people who visited our stores, to all those
who believed in our dreams and my
family and friends who stood by me,
who continue to believe in me.*

Contents

Acknowledgements

This book is a synergistic product of many minds. It is not a chronology of events, but a collection of ideas at work. Capturing the diverse elements had its own set of challenges, as a book essentially has a linear format, is passive by nature and forces the reader to go with the pace of the author. In order to improvise on the narrative, we tried to make it an interactive reading experience by requesting some of our colleagues, associates and acquaintances to share their views, comments and judgements.

More than a hundred people were interviewed during the various stages of writing the book. Many more shared their thoughts informally and gave suggestions for enhancing the manuscript. And although everyone has not been featured here, it in no way reduces the value of all that they shared.

Within our organisation, Prashant Desai incubated the idea of writing this book and supported it with information and inputs wherever required. Others — including, but not limited to Sanjeev Agrawal, K.K. Rathi and G.R. Venkatesh — provided timely feedback and insights.

We would like to acknowledge the younger generation, Ashni, Avni, Nishita and Vivek for the fresh thinking that they brought into this book. Among my friends and family, Abhay Kumat and Anju Poddar went through the numerous versions of the manuscript and gave valuable comments on it.

A large portion of the research that went into writing this book was based on company documents and reports, as well as Indian and foreign media sources. And over the years, the several books and articles that have shaped our organisation and its values, have been reflected in various parts of the book — including the names of chapters. If we have inadvertently failed to cite any published works or other sources from which we have benefited in telling our story, we apologise in advance.

This book wouldn't have been complete, had it not been for the enthusiasm and deep involvement of the young team at the publishers'. In Rupa & Co., we found a publishing house that believes in speed and promptness as much as we do, a trait not very common in the publishing industry.

Last but not the least, we have numerous colleagues and business partners who collectively serve millions of customers and enjoy the trust of thousands of our shareholders. And it was the assurance and loyalty of our customers who visit our stores and approve of our business, which gave us the confidence that our story *must* be shared with you.

Foreword

As the idea to write this book emerged, I constantly questioned and argued with my father about the purpose of writing the book so soon. I felt that the story had only just begun and there could be even greater times in the future to share it. But after much discussion, I now understand the relevance of communicating the story to the *potential* India of tomorrow. I realise that India needs role models who will make it believe that it can happen right here, in this country. My generation needs figures that we do not epitomise but relate and connect with. We need the story of ordinary people who have made extraordinary things happen during *our* times.

This book is indeed very special! It is special not only because it is the story of my father, but also because it dares me and my generation to dream. It gives me the courage to aspire, and believe that we can create and change things. This simple story of a *dukandaar*, who learnt while doing, makes me believe that with conviction and self-belief no dream is distant. And to conquer one's dreams one only needs passion.

The musings presented here are no images of perfection. In fact, the experience of reading this book may leave you a little bewildered. For example, Dad has always believed in the power of spending instead of saving. He strongly believes that the more you spend the more you aspire and therefore earn. And the mantra 'rewrite rules and retain values' may puzzle you further.

I hope this book will probe, perplex and provoke you and also challenge your accepted notions and beliefs.

Beyond everything, the book is about relationships. Relationships that have made it all happen. Relationships my father has shared with his customers, shareholders, colleagues, investors, partners, suppliers, well-wishers, his friends and us.

Kishore Biyani to many will be the man who created the dais for modern retail in India. To others, he will always be an inspiration, a leader yet a learner, and a passionate knowledge worker.

Ashni Biyani
30th January 2007
Mumbai

Made in India

*'Sometimes, we a nation of billion people,
think like a nation of million people.'*

A.P.J. ABDUL KALAM

I

It was a Thursday morning that started like no other. At 7:30 in the morning, I received a call from Sadashiv Nayak, head of our operations in the western region informing me that there was a long queue of customers waiting outside the Big Bazaar in Lower Parel, Mumbai. The store was supposed to open at eight. I decided to check the situation first hand, but even before I could get started, similar calls from Bangalore, Gurgaon, and Kolkata informed me of long queues of customers waiting outside Big Bazaar stores at those places as well. By the time I was about to leave, news came in that things were fast getting out of hand at many locations. In Kolkata, where one of our stores is located on the V.I.P. Road that connects the city to the airport, eager customers had spilled on to the streets and blocked the airport traffic. Our second outlet in Kolkata is located within a residential compound called Hiland Park. There our managers had started to pull down the shutters after residents of the locality complained that they couldn't get in or out of the compound due to the large crowds blocking the entrance. A similar step was being taken at V.I.P. Road as well, but Kolkata being Kolkata, customers had started banging on the shutters and heckling the staff. The police, who had earlier insisted that the stores be shut down, was now unable to control the situation and told our staff to reopen the store.

By 10 a.m., I managed to enter the Big Bazaar at Lower Parel. Spread across 55,000 square feet, the store attracts a few thousand customers on any regular day. The store was now bursting with ten thousand people inside and an equal number waiting outside the store. Our attempt at appealing to customers with rock-bottom prices at Big Bazaar stores had resulted in a situation that even we couldn't have imagined.

Over the years, we have been offering special promotions and offers at Big Bazaar during Diwali. Last Diwali, these offers had elicited an unprecedented response from customers. The sales team was fairly enthused about it and had suggested that we organise an event on which customers could benefit from even better promotions and offers. We had then decided to do it sometime in January or February when retail sales are typically sluggish.

The 26th of January being the Republic Day, is a national holiday when most people spend time at home with their family. This provided us with an ideal opportunity to add more vitality and celebrations for customers. Some smart sourcing deals were struck with a large number of small vendors and a media blitzkrieg was launched promoting the *Sabse Sasta Din* or Maha Savings Day on radio and in newspapers.

RAJAN MALHOTRA*

The brief was very simple, 'Create a day without a season that truly belongs to us every year.' The Republic Day was quite close and it seemed to be ideal. I suggested the catchphrase, '26 ko 26' and thus the target of Rs 26 crore of sales in one single day was set — a feat and a number not projected by any mathematical equation but a number born simply out of a desire to unlock our minds and do something truly extraordinary.

---

*Rajan Malhotra is Head, Big Bazaar. He joined the company in 2000.

As always all the teams — marketing, operations, IT, category management — went about what's called the 'war drill.' Yet to be honest there was always that nagging doubt in our mind that we had chosen a window of just twenty-four hours. What if the sales did not take off? There was hardly any time to correct our plans, if the response from customers didn't live up to our expectations. I remember discussing the same at our review meeting on Monday. But as usual, KB assured us that all trends were positive and we would have an exceptional day. We made the mistake of not believing in him fully.

The result was both alarming and astounding. Within a few hours the anxiety and excitement had culminated into a fear. The focus soon shifted from meeting sales targets to the safety and protection of thousands of customers who were inside our stores. While our colleagues at the stores are trained to handle chaotic situations on a daily basis, no one was really prepared to handle such a mammoth crowd.

At almost all locations the police came in to control the crowds waiting outside the stores. And within a couple of hours of business most stores had to be closed down so that the situation didn't go completely out of hand. At Koramangala in Bangalore, attempts at shutting down the store failed. This prompted the local police official to unilaterally announce on the public address system that the sale had been extended for another day.

Each one of us in the organisation was surprised by the response from customers. High-ticket items like televisions, mobile phones and DVD players flew off the shelves like vegetables. Customers were carrying the four-page ads that we had released the previous morning. Nobody wanted to return empty-handed. They had read about the offers and they wanted to get each of the deals mentioned in the ads.

Bizarre incidents happened as well. At Lower Parel, some customers tried to bribe the security guard fifty rupees, to let them enter the store. Elsewhere, a customer standing in the queue wanted to go to the washroom inside the store. He was allowed in, but soon more customers figured out that going to the washroom was a smart way of jumping the queue and entering the store. They then had to be told that there was a long queue outside the washroom as well. At the Kandivili outlet in Mumbai, customers fell head over heels on a ready-to-eat Buy One Get One (BOGO) offer on *basmati* rice. The situation deteriorated to such an extent that one of our staff members was injured and had to be rushed to a nearby hospital.

By the time I reached Lower Parel that morning, I noticed Outside Broadcast (OBC) vans being parked outside the mall. Television channels were soon beaming live images of the crowd. The *Sabse Sasta Din* had turned into a topic of national importance covered by the media almost to the fervour of a one-day cricket match. Next morning almost every national and local daily reported the excitement.

RETAIL ROCKS – BIG BAZAAR SALE A BIG HIT
Times of India, 27 January 2006

Sharad Verma was stunned. Ever since the marketing executive from Delhi stepped off the bus to head towards the Big Bazaar outlet in Kandivili, all he could see was a sea of heads. Hundreds of people had been waiting for more than four hours for their turn to just get into the store. But around 1:30 p.m., unable to control the unprecedented traffic, the store managers downed the shutters for the day.

Many had to turn back disappointed that they couldn't avail of any of the mouth-watering deals. As for the lot that did, they lugged home flat TVs priced at Rs 5,890, mobiles for Rs 1,399 and designer sofas for Rs 15,999. In the end, Big Bazaar is said to have clocked about Rs 30 crore — once again the highest sales in a day.

By 26th January afternoon, we decided to continue this promotion for two more days. Again large number of customers turned up, but we managed to do a better job. Barricades were erected to manage the movement of customers, tokens were issued and refreshments were provided for customers waiting in the queues outside the store.

II

Post January 2006, the story of Big Bazaar can be described in two phases — the one before and the one after the *Sabse Sasta Din*. At the store-level, the 26th January experience gave all of us a lot of confidence. Going by the number of customers who visited our stores, it was evident that given the right environment and a correct emotional connect with customers, anything was possible. After this, no one in our organisation thinks any sales target is impossible to achieve.

There are a couple of emotions that determine shopping behaviour. The most fundamental of them are greed, altruism, fear and envy. Greed drives a customer to purchase more than what he or she needs. A wide range of options, better products and lower prices generate that increased desire to purchase. Often, a customer would consider it a good opportunity to buy more than what she needs and to gift others as well. Higher purchase is also driven by the fear that the current price offer may not be available for long and so the product has to be purchased right away. And envy sets in when one sees others buying and making the best out of a deal. *Sabse Sasta Din* was successful because we were able to effectively capitalise on all of these emotions. The prices were great but they were on offer only for a day. Customers noticed everyone else — friends, colleagues, neighbours heading to Big Bazaar and they didn't want the opportunity to pass by. With all these emotions working in complete harmony, the stage was set for a huge response.

But more than the quantum of sales, what seemed significant to me was that this incident marked the arrival of a new set of customers into the modern retail stores in India. Marketers are prone to classifying consumers into various categories, sub-categories, income strata, etc. For us, every Indian who has some aspirations is a potential customer.

We divide India into three sets — India One, India Two and India Three. These groups can be understood as the consuming class, the serving class and the struggling class. Our studies show that India One or the consuming class constitutes only fourteen percent of the country's population. Till recently all modern retail formats, including Big Bazaar, were attracting customers mostly from this segment. Most of these customers have a substantial disposable income and form part of what are usually called the upper middle and the lower middle class.

India Two or the serving class includes people like drivers, household helps, office peons, liftmen, washermen, etc. They are the people who make life easier and more comfortable for the consuming class or India One. For every India One, there are at least three India Twos, making up almost fifty-five percent of the population. But India One doesn't care to pay India Two too well (think of how many times you have got a salary increment and how many times your driver has got an increment). While their numbers are huge they still have very little disposable income to spend on buying aspirational products and services.

Then there is the struggling class or India Three, which lives a hand-to-mouth existence and cannot afford to even aspire for a better living. Unfortunately, this segment will continue to be on the peripheries of the consumption cycle in India for quite a few years to come. Their needs cannot be addressed by the existing business models.

Among the two relevant sets of potential consumers, we have also noticed that the master and the serving class employee never shop at the same store. While the lower middle class visits hypermarkets and discount chains, the upper middle class frequents department stores and speciality chains as well as supermarkets. And even though India Two may be buying some of the same products that India One consumes — albeit in smaller quantities — they never visit the modern retail chains. For them, the clean and shiny environment of modern retail stores creates the perception that such stores are too expensive and exclusive; and are therefore not meant for them. India Two tends to feel alienated in environments frequented by India One. It is probably a unique Indian phenomenon.

What was exceptional about 26th January 2006 at Big Bazaar was that for the first time it had attracted India Two and that too in very large numbers. In the preceding months, we had spent considerable time at various *chawls* and slums of Mumbai, including Dharavi, trying to understand the needs, aspirations and buying behaviour of the residents. Among the things we noticed was that India Two moves and finds a lot of comfort in crowds. They are not individualistic. There is a definite need for them to do new things only if they see someone from their community doing it. What came as a pleasant surprise was that Big Bazaar was finally able to attract this segment on the *Sabse Sasta Din*. They shed their inhibitions and decided to make the best of the deals that were on offer. More and more customers from this segment gathered at Big Bazaar through the day. It confirmed that a new era of consumerism was finally setting in.

RAMA BIJAPURKAR*

In India, most of us are not prepared for the consumerism that's setting in this country. We underestimate how many people are going to fly and that's why our airports get jammed. We underestimate how many people will speak on phones for how many billions of minutes and therefore our cell phone networks are always congested. We are not prepared for the force of consumerism which is unfolding.

III

The most challenging and exciting time to live in, is on cusp of this change wherein a huge, multicultural India is transforming

---

*Rama Bijapurkar is an independent market consultant and a board member of several reputed companies.

from a socialist economy to a consumption-led economy. However, we have not yet been able to comprehend the scope and depth of this change. Often, we do not even accept it. That's why we are taken off-guard when an entirely new set of people get added to the consuming class. Earlier, we used to stand in queues at the bus stop or at the railway reservation counter. Now, we stand in a queue at the airport, because no one could conceive that so many people will choose to fly. Earlier, we used to drive ordinary cars to office. Now we drive better cars, but it takes more time because road conditions have deteriorated. The roads were built keeping in mind that only a small elite will be driving cars.

Yet, the fact remains that changing demographic profiles, increasing income levels, urbanisation, technology, globalisation and a free flow of ideas from within and outside the country, is bringing about a dramatic shift in consumer tastes and preferences. Customer segments are maturing faster than ever. Even as some Indians become sophisticated shoppers, tens of millions of less experienced but no less avid consumers are joining the fray every year. As retailers and marketers, we not only have to acknowledge this change but also stay a step ahead of the evolution curve of the Indian market. In a young nation our job is to develop new ideas and create new delivery formats that can cater to the huge mass of consumers. Going forward, our growth will be based not on the physical assets we have, but on the ideas and solutions that we generate to capture the imagination of the Indian consumer. And when these ideas spread like wildfire across the nation, we will be able to leverage the power of consumption that is unfolding amidst us.

However, what sets India apart is the diversity and uniqueness of the Indian market. On any given week, somewhere, some of our countrymen are celebrating a festival about which most of us may not have a single clue. The rice we eat, the apparel that our women wear, the dialects we speak, change every hundred kilometres in our country. There are also a lot of conflicting trends and paradoxes that are evident across the country. Logic and emotion, individuality and social feeling, poverty and affluence, life and lifestyle, value and indulgence, and the past and the future simultaneously coexist in India. And all these paradoxes converge to make India what it is.

To the external world, this harmonious coexistence of seeming contradictions is one of the most confusing aspects of the Indian consumer market. But to me it signifies our country's openness to change and its ability to add new dimensions to its social structure without losing the old ones. This opens up new and unique opportunities as well as brings forth challenges for marketers and retailers.

Few can deny that India today provides the single biggest consumption opportunity in the world that is yet largely untapped. Given the new era of growth we are entering, the per capita income is almost set to double in the country. By 2010, almost half of our citizens will be in the working age group of twenty to fifty-four years. A youthful, exuberant generation, bred on success will not only drive productivity but also set a spiralling effect on consumption and income generation. A young nation is willing to work harder, earn higher and spend more on buying goods and services.

In fact, this change is no longer restricted to the large cities. Today it's fashionable to talk about the booming mid-size cities like Nagpur, Surat, Vadodara, Vijaywada and Indore. But our experience in running modern retail outlets in even smaller towns like Sangli, Panipat, Palakkad, Durgapur or Ambala shows that this change is far more conspicuous at these places.

And this is a trend that is evident not only at shopping malls. If one considers Bollywood, cricket and prime-time television to be the barometers of change and popular culture in India, this trend becomes far more apparent. The most popular shows on Indian television today are undoubtedly the contest shows. And behind the glitz and glamour of these shows, one can find that most of the winners are people from small towns, rather than the metros. They come with the confidence to win a big title in the city of dreams, Mumbai. The desire to be a part of the get-rich-quick model, the instant-fame route is as popular in small towns as in the metros. The popularity of movies like *Rang De Basanti* proves that a young India believes in change and more importantly, that *they* can affect it. When it comes to cricket, in stark contrast to what it was even five years back, most of the members of the Indian cricket team come from small cities and towns.

Underlying these trends, I feel, are two undercurrents that are sweeping through young India — confidence and change. Confidence, that lends itself to self-belief and a total lack of inhibitions to achieve any dream; and a willingness to change, or the desire to rise above one's origins. And it is the young generation of Indians who are playing a pivotal role in driving these trends.

My parents were born in a nation that was about to gain independence. I was born in a nation that was experimenting with socialism. The new generation has grown up in a liberalised economy and has seen India winning in every arena. Be it in business, information technology, sports, or beauty pageants, they have been witness to the era where India is emerging as a global powerhouse. The current generation is therefore simultaneously more proud about being Indian, and more modern when it comes to their lifestyles, than their predecessors. In essence, they are far more confident of their place in the world. This is a generation that feels that everything is within their reach and aspires for it. And this is true for everyone, whether they live in large metros or small towns.

It is this age group that is setting off the virtuous cycle of consumption-led economic growth and prosperity in our country. I call this paradigm shift, the 3-C theory: Confidence and Change bringing in an unprecedented era of Consumption.

Increase in consumption is driving manufacturing, thereby creating more jobs and income for the entire population. The change is far more dramatic when one considers that with the popularity of modern retail, the market for packaged and value-added food products is expanding at a fast pace. This is providing the much-needed boost to value creation in agro-products. In turn there is more wealth-creation and rise in consumer demand even in the smaller towns and semi-urban centres.

However, to leverage on this trend, marketers and retailers in India have to understand and interpret the Indian consumer accurately. This wave of change, confidence and consumption cannot be compared with anything that has happened in any country or region in the world. India is developing in a way and in an era that has no parallel in the world. Indian consumers are far from converting into copies of their western counterparts, as many would like to believe. A few similarities may surface as they are continually exposed to modern retail, global media and transnational trends. But our experience in retailing suggests that Indian consumers — particularly the younger generation — will continue to embrace the values of family and community and live the Indian way. Consumers here, unlike others, demand ideas and solutions that are uniquely Indian. We have to understand, interpret, attract and deliver to the Indian consumer in a way that takes into account the Indian context. The concept of 'Indian-ness' has to be understood if one wants to attract the maximum number of consumers.

When we started this company, we believed in this core value of Indian-ness. For us, Indian-ness is not about *swadeshi*, it is about believing in the Indian way of doing things. We wanted to understand and interpret India in a way that no one else had done. We wanted to rewrite the rules of catering to Indian consumers. Our stated objective from day one was: Rewrite Rules, Retain Values.

IV

There are no given rules as such in business. I believe that one has to make his or her rules and rewrite the existing ones. However, during our early days most people found this unacceptable. When we started off, most thought that we are a crazy bunch trying our luck at business, or worse, some fly-by-night operators waiting to con investors at the stock markets. Hardly anyone was willing to appreciate our way of working. When they talked or wrote about our company, they either got it wrong or just made fun of us.

In a business where the other players were among the biggest Indian business houses — the Tatas, Goenkas, Piramals, Rahejas — we were seen as a small-time Marwari *bania* company trying to reinvent the wheel. Unlike our competitors, we neither had financial muscle nor business experience or any legacy to boast of. All we had was lots of passion and self-belief. We took large risks, made a number of mistakes, faltered on the way and learned things while doing it.

THE MAN WHO WOULD BE KING
M. Rajshekhar, *BusinessWorld*, 28 October 2002

Kishore Biyani isn't quite the poster boy of India's organised retail industry. He lives on its periphery, ever willing to take extraordinary bets. His peers dismiss him as a compulsive risk-taker — he was the first who dared to try out the hypermarket model. The press, fed up with his recalcitrance to meet or talk, largely ignores him. He is seldom invited for retail seminars. But Biyani doesn't care. He is quite content being the outsider who has built up a Rs 220 crore business in the nascent Indian retail sector.

At investor conferences, trade body meetings or in the media, we were ignored or just written off. Slowly we accepted the fact that there would be plenty of disbelievers if we are starting something new or trying something that is quite unique. We were leaving the security and comfort of the base camp and getting into an entirely new and emerging business. The objective was to become the trailblazers, the pathfinders and open new possibilities and new markets. It was only natural that there would be plenty of cynics.

In fact, it was encouraging to find that most people were dismissing us — it was a proof of the fact that we were doing things truly differently. I chose to become an entrepreneur because I wanted to do things *my* way. Changing my belief and my way of working simply because that's what others wanted was never an option.

It was not just the cynics who could have discouraged us. On our journey, we faced plenty of roadblocks. At times we would make deliberate mistakes and at times some not so deliberate ones. There were teething financial crunches that almost put our expansion plans to rest. On a number of occasions our understanding of the market and our strategies went wrong. Looking back, I feel that the sense of achievement came only because we faced so many obstacles and overcame them all one by one. Without these persistent difficulties and unrelenting critics, this journey would not have been worth sharing with you.

RENUKA RAMNATH*

Imagine a situation where you are working with a fairly ordinary set of people and have a mediocre balance sheet. There are also a good many disbelievers in your strategy and people waiting to write you off. Under such circumstances you go ahead and rewrite the rules, simply because you just *know* that your lifetime opportunity is staring at you and it will place you on an invincible platform. Kishore Biyani did just that and that's where my respect for him goes up.

He is not like the traditional guy who is very articulate, comes into a meeting surrounded by three MBAs and makes slick PowerPoint presentations. This man will come dressed like a *dukandaar*, alone with no airs, no presentations and operates from part intuition and part gut-feel. He has

*Renuka Ramnath is the Managing Director of ICICI Ventures. It was the first private equity fund to invest in the company in 1999.

tremendous courage of conviction, and backs these with phenomenal speed and personal energy. And he doesn't look for endorsement from twenty other people.

In fact, I find that having a lot of critics actually helped us to continuously be on our toes and improve upon what we were doing. Some of our biggest disbelievers were often people in our own industry and a few people in the financial community. However, Pantaloon wouldn't have been what it is today, had it not been for these people. They pushed us hard to perform better and prove them wrong.

Way back in the early Nineties, when the first retail chain came up in Mumbai, we used to be a small trouser manufacturer. We had approached them at that point to stock our brands. Since they stocked mostly foreign labels in those days, they flatly refused to keep our brands. I think that was the day we started to explore whether we could open our own retail chain. Many years later, the owners of this retail chain once again refused to give space to our store at a sprawling mall that they built in Mumbai. This incident further prompted us to explore the option of setting up a real estate fund that could invest in development of retail real estate. Then, there is a much respected lady from a large business house who used to refer to our chain as 'dirty stores.' And a self-styled consultant, who hardly had any *locus standi* in the industry or any achievement worth talking about, made it a point to rubbish us in the media every time he got an opportunity. Now, it's amusing to see how many of these people have changed their opinion about us.

Anyway, we never looked for endorsement from people within the industry. For us, it was the customer who mattered. We believe it is the customer alone who decides whether we are successful or not. Neither we nor our competitors or investors can decide our success. From what we should sell and how to sell it, to which formats are successful and which are not, everything is decided only by customers. So, the primary rule of our business is that the customer is always right. Any product, any format, any strategy that the customer disapproved of was changed or closed down.

Every time we have taken a decision we focussed on the simple aspects keeping our customer in mind. I emphasise the word 'simple' because I believe that business *is* simple. Most people try to make it complex because they are trained to think that way. In fact, many try to justify their jobs by *making* things complex. We are a nation of shopkeepers and there are a billion people to sell to. Selling garments, grocery and household stuff cannot be anything but simple. It is definitely not rocket science. Retailing is a simple act of buying and selling. Through this book I hope to take you through our journey and show you examples of how keeping things simple helped us build a winning proposition.

I think a lot of these beliefs came from my having grown up in a middle class family. A very successful idea of having a live *chakki* (wheat-grinder) within our store came from my memory of how my mother shopped. She used to buy grains at one shop and then take it to another that had a grinding machine to get it ground into wheat in her presence. She was never comfortable with packaged grain — she preferred to touch, smell and feel the wheat grains before she bought them. And while the maid made the dough, she baked the *rotis* herself. Looking around, I found that she wasn't the only one; pretty much most housewives preferred doing things this way. When it comes to her family, there are certain things a homemaker prefers to do herself. These lessons helped evolve the various sections within Food Bazaar, including one where all staples are sold loose. It's now good to see that many of these ideas have become standard features at most of the supermarkets that are coming up.

In fact, women have provided some of the best insights and inputs on building our retailing business. My wife and daughters continue to be my biggest critics, and always have suggestions and feedback on how we can improve our stores. A lot of women professionals are among my most reliable sounding boards for every decision that I make. Women are not just avid shoppers; I have found women to be better than men in a lot of areas like eye for detail, understanding social implications of business and interpreting the softer and emotional issues related to customer behaviour. My friend, Anju Poddar has provided me with some of the most interesting insights and inputs that have helped us design our strategy for women consumers.

ANJU PODDAR*

Something Kishore likes doing is visiting different stores. And that is not for shopping — he hates spending on himself. It doesn't matter whether the store he is visiting is a Pantaloons store or not. But whenever he is at any store, he gets busy watching people from a distance — how they shop, what they wear and what they buy. He will notice the most innocuous things among people and would then try to seek an answer to why a particular

---

*Anju Poddar is a close friend of Kishore and has known him for several years. She is also on the board of Directors of Pantaloon Retail.

shopper bought something or behaved in a particular manner. He has hundreds of questions running through his mind at any point of time. He would then call up people and start quizzing them on things that he couldn't find a logical answer to.

During the early days, we used to celebrate every small thing — Kishore's first appearance on a magazine cover, his first award, his first television appearance. That has now become a thing of past, but I don't think fame or fortune has changed him in any way. He is still as simple, as astute and as shy as he was seven years back. He still likes to listen, speak and understand every person around him. And he is always looking for new things to learn. My cook, of course, doesn't have a very high opinion of him. When the first Big Bazaar opened in Hyderabad he came back saying, 'Your friend doesn't make any money. The sugar he sells at his shop goes for fifteen rupees a kilo but he sells it at Rs 5!'

Till date, most of my Sundays are spent outside shopping malls watching human behaviour. Watching people behave and interact with others and their surroundings is probably my second biggest passion, the first of course, being Hindi films. I have tried to make everyone in my organisation an observer of customer behaviour. And now, some of the best business ideas come from our colleagues at the shop floor. They are trained to study and understand customer needs. My job is to transform these observations into actionable ideas.

IREENA VITTAL*

I think, Kishore will agree that it's too early to decide whether he is successful or not. Competition is still emerging and the consumer is going to change very rapidly. The game has just begun. But what is interesting is that every maverick challenger that I have seen in any industry and in any country is pretty much like Kishore. They all have a similar pattern.

One, they always start with the customer — they are customer driven as opposed to product driven. Second, they take a huge amount of pride in writing and rewriting rules. Third, there is a fine balance between confidence in making choices and humility in learning. And that third to me is more often the number one. The few people I have seen who are interesting and have set industry standards have these common characteristics and so it is with Kishore. Once he takes a decision he moves fast. Yet at the same time, he is always looking around for learning and is humble enough to seek it.

The interesting thing about Kishore is that he is extremely conscious of the cultural context of India and is willing to try out a hell lot of new things. The question is will he survive in the long run? Retail is not just customer delight. Innovation matters but over time so does scale, cost structures and execution at the store level. So he has to keep improving things and be vigilant.

---

*Ireena Vittal is a Partner at the consultancy firm, McKinsey & Co. She heads the firm's retail practice in India.

Everyone in our organisation believes in the continuous process of learning, unlearning and relearning. Rather than over-emphasising on hard numbers and figures, we laid a lot of stress on softer aspects like self-development and thought leadership. Internally, the emphasis has been on helping colleagues and co-workers realise their true potential. Now, that is helping us creating a culture of innovation and creativity. We have taken a lot of steps that allow people to approach challenges in a creative way and work in a seamless manner. I wouldn't suggest that we are an ideal organisation, but I think we have made the beginning towards building one.

SHIVANAND MANKEKAR*

The key to being a successful entrepreneur is having an ability to innovate and an ability to execute these innovations really well. What sets KB apart is that he has these abilities in plenty. In fact, many people often worry whether he tries to do too many innovations. But I don't see it as an area of concern because all his innovations are built around his core business. There is a clear logic and method behind every idea, which he then implements with unwavering conviction.

The key to success in the retail business in India was firstly getting the model right and then scaling up quickly before the competition began copying the model. When we met KB for the first time he said, 'Retail is like riding a bicycle

---

*Shivanand Mankekar is a visiting Professor of Finance at Mumbai's Jamnalal Bajaj Institute of Management Studies. He is also an individual investor in the company.

uphill, if you stop pedalling, you will slide down,' clearly indicating that he understood the need to scale up fast. The opportunity that knocks at one's door doesn't remain there forever. KB's strategy has been aggressive but he has always taken calculated risks rather than playing mindless gambles. That strategy has paid off and put him way ahead of the competition.

V

Pantaloon Retail was incorporated in October 1987. The company then had a different name and could manufacture two hundred trousers per day. In August 1997, we forayed into modern retail with an initial investment of Rs 30 lakh and opened a Pantaloons family store in Gariahat, Kolkata. Four years later in 2001, we opened the first Big Bazaar store. Subsequently, we launched a number of retail formats and got into different businesses in the consumption space.

It was during this period that we were successfully able to rewrite quite a few rules of retailing. One of the most significant was the way in which we designed our retail stores. The most obvious question being in the business of retail is, how can one not get inspired from the US based Wal-Mart, one of the largest companies in the world? Fortunately for me, the first time I got to visit the United States was in 2003, to speak at a panel discussion at the Harvard Business School. This was almost two years after we had launched Big Bazaar and it was the first time I got a chance to visit an American retail chain.

While it was improbable that we would get inspired from Wal-Mart, or for that matter any other retail chain, I couldn't help but get inspired by Sam Walton, the iconic founder of the chain. I have learned some of the most enduring lessons of business from a heavily underlined and dog-eared copy of the classic *Made in America*. Sam Walton was the original master of rewriting rules — he never followed the existing patterns of his time. He studied the market and developed a model that truly suited the American context. Taking my lessons from him, I couldn't have blankly copied the American model for the Indian context.

While designing our Big Bazaar stores the core idea has been to merge the look and feel of the *mandis* with modern retail's features like quality, choice and convenience. The Indian customer needs an indigenous solution to her shopping needs — that gives her the best value for money in an environment where she is comfortable. At the same time the heterogeneity of our country doesn't provide the luxury of following a cookie-cutter approach for setting up a store. Each and every store in India needs to be customised after taking into account the diverse culture, tastes and preferences of every city or locality that we want to set up the store in.

HARVARD BUSINESS SCHOOL CASE STUDY*

Though Biyani initially had been derided by many peers and analysts for his unconventional ideas, by 2005 he was dubbed the Indian 'Rajah of Retail' (*Business Today*, 13 March 2005). He was seen as the trendsetter in Indian retailing, having proven his ability to pull consumers who

---

*Professor Ananth Raman & Senior Researcher Laura Winig, Global Research Group, Harvard Business School prepared this case study on Big Bazaar. It was presented on 6 May 2006.

shopped in traditional bazaars into his Big Bazaar stores. Most Indian consumers were accustomed to shopping at the small neighbourhood stores or purchasing from street hawkers; only a small fraction of the population had tried and become comfortable with the 'organised' retail stores. To persuade consumers to try Big Bazaar, the company incorporated elements of the bazaar experience into its stores. For example, while shopping for food grains locally, consumers usually touched the products to assess quality. Hence, in addition to offering pre-packaged grains, Big Bazaar stores were designed to offer loose, self-serve grains that consumers could touch.

Within nine years of opening our first big Pantaloons retail outlet, we now have around two hundred outlets in thirty-four Indian cities covering almost four million square feet. Through our retail business we sell almost everything from food and grocery, apparel, footwear, furniture to consumer electronics, home products, books, music, medicines and communication products. That constitutes nearly seventy percent of a person's consumption basket. These are available through multiple delivery formats like hypermarkets, supermarkets, seamless malls, fashion destinations, speciality stores and an online portal.

While retail continues to be our core business, we now have presence across the broader consumption space as well. We operate restaurants and entertainment centres. We manage venture capital funds that are being invested in building shopping centres and market cities as well as developing indigenous brands. We are setting up a large logistics network and developing retail media properties across the country. We are now about to launch insurance products and consumer finance products. All these initiatives including our retail business have now come under the umbrella of Future Group.

I think we have achieved some amount of success in what we have done. Now, even many of our critics perceive us to be a serious player in the business. Though the number of critics hasn't changed, their questions have. These days I am often asked whether I am planning to sell off the company anytime soon!

I haven't yet figured out why this question is never asked to the inheritors and owners of the large business houses. I have found this question being asked only to first-generation entrepreneurs. If I have put in my life's effort into what I am most passionate about, why would I sell it? We are here for the long run and the knowledge which we have accumulated about Indian customers will continue to be the biggest differentiating factor with respect to our competitors. I do not foresee any reason why we will exit or sell any businesses that are successful and have the potential to grow further.

RAMA BIJAPURKAR*

The first time I met Kishore, I said to him in surprise, 'You really aren't my type! I can't see what areas we can work in together...' He asked me to come and see his office first. I did. And I saw one of his silent story presentations. I was hooked.

---

*Rama Bijapurkar is an independent market consultant and a board member of several reputed companies.

Later I said to him that I couldn't see what value I was delivering to him, so he should stop paying me. He heard me out and then delivered his characteristic punch that it is not your job to deliver value to me, but it's my job to extract value from you.

He has met the rich, the famous, the dumb, the competitor's competitor, the worldly, the unworldly, the gurus, the whole goddamn world. He is open to meeting anybody who has something new to offer. What he really does is put himself in a position where he exposes himself to various people and ideates and incubates, shapes and refines, tests and challenges, his own thinking. What he is essentially looking for, is people who can stimulate, engage and challenge him. And that's the role I play, and learn enormously in the process too. It is lots of fun. Though a bit enervating at times!

To come up with new ideas one also needs informational resources. Most people get their informational resources from the west. Kishore gets them from here in India. He is an extremely strong observer and he is almost paranoid about losing touch with the man on the street. His informational resources come from watching people at shops, temples, homes and on the street. And based on his observation and intuition he builds his business ideas.

There is always a confluence of events for every entrepreneur. At that point the entrepreneur decides to go ahead of his time with the belief that the economy will catch up. He follows a process of hypothetical development and envisioning the future. You may later say he was lucky but I think people like Kishore took a leveraged bet on the Indian economy.

For Kishore there was the choice of whether he wanted to sail one boat at a time or launch a fleet with the belief that the wind will catch up someday. In hindsight, things have only got better for him, the economy is growing, consumerism is setting in and whole lot of new players are now attracted to this sector. Now whether he saw all this coming or it just came together God only knows. But there is definitely a plan in the whole madness. I did ask him this once though, and he said that with each step higher he climbed, he saw a little further, and built a little further!

In the following chapters I will take you through my journey first as an adolescent and then as an entrepreneur. I will also try to explain what has been our way of doing things. There are critics who say that we have been lucky to have achieved whatever we have till now. My reply is, yes we have been lucky. We were fortunate enough to be in the right business, at the right time, in the right country.

Built from Scratch

'Strength lies in differences, not in similarities.'

STEPHEN COVEY

I

My grandfather, Late Bansi Lal Biyani arrived in the city then known as Bombay in the summer of 1935. He came from Nimbi, a nondescript village in Nagaur district of Rajasthan, located almost 137 kilometres from Jodhpur, on the borders of the Thar Desert. Apart from an old temple dedicated to the Hindu god Hanuman, and a huge fort complex originally built by the Nagvanshi kings in the fourth century, located within fifty kilometres, there's nothing else worth mentioning about Nimbi. However, the district town is better known for its annual animal fair held in the month of February. The fair at Nagaur is considered to be second only to the more famous one held in Pushkar. My first and only visit to the fair was at the age of ten years. It seemed to be an eclectic gathering of men and beasts, brisk trading and keen competition in the best traditions of this town. Held in the outskirts of the town, I remember watching camel races, cock fights, puppet shows, folk dancing, tugs-of-war and a host of other activities. Cows, oxen, horses and camels were on sale. As the sun set, local folk musicians filled up the atmosphere with melodies that would resound far and wide across the tranquil desert sands. As I would realise later, commerce is never the *raison d'etre* of Indian bazaars, they are more of a social mélange.

Since the mid-eighteenth century, the village, much like the rest of Rajasthan, had seen a steady emigration of the Marwari *Maheshwari bania* (trading) community to the big cities across the country in search of prosperity and fortune. My grandfather must have been in his early twenties when he decided to leave the village and head towards Mumbai. He must have been drawn by the success of the other villagers who had moved to the big city earlier. With some help from fellow community members, he set up his first business, a shop selling dhotis and saris in Vithawadi, in central Mumbai. I don't have very strong memories of my grandfather, but he was much like the men of his generation — he believed in hard work, sincerity and ethics. He had the wherewithal to establish himself in a completely new environment. As the shop started to take off, he called all his six sons to Mumbai to help him in the business. They were all permanently settled in the city by the early 1950s.

But those must have been tough times with the government playing big brother in any business that one planned to get into. Import restrictions and quotas used to make a mockery of one's entrepreneurial spirits. However, he had grown up in the deserts and wasn't one to give up easily. He started a partnership concern, Comtex Industries that procured and marketed polyester knitted shirts. Around the same time he also managed to bag the sole distributorship of Ashoka Industries, a textile company based in Nepal.

I was born on 9th of August, 1961, the second son of Shri Laxmi Narayan Biyani and Shrimati Godavari Biyani. The year after I was born, the family set up its second business in synthetic furnishing and for some, yet unexplained reason, named it Messrs Kishore Kumar Biyani. My family members tell me that my horoscope was an extremely encouraging one, so they were quite sure I will be successful. Fortunately or unfortunately, I haven't yet bothered to look at that horoscope.

The family had first settled down in Borivili, a northern suburb and subsequently moved to Zaveri Bazaar, the old business district located in the heart of Mumbai. A year after I was born, they moved to an apartment in Jeevan Vihar in Malabar Hills. Like most other families of those days, it was a joint family. My grandparents along with my five uncles, aunts and my parents lived in the same building. I grew up among twelve cousins and siblings. Most of us went to the nearby Manav Mandir High School.

Besides all the children in the family there were scores of youngsters from the hundred-odd families living in the same residential compound, so I was never short of friends. A mediocre student, I don't remember ever coming first or failing any major exam. My school hours were fairly uneventful as my focus was more on going back home to play cricket.

A common preoccupation was cricket or gully cricket, as it is called now. We made our own rules and had our own bit of improvisation — whether playing in the parking space of the compound or on the terrace. It involved tennis balls and under-arm bowling and it was fiercely competitive. Placing bets and gaining or losing a few rupees every evening wasn't exactly uncommon. Occasionally, we would go to a nearby cricket ground as part of the housing society's cricket team. I considered myself to be somewhat of an all-rounder, and as my elder brother Vijayji still points out, accepting defeat even then was difficult for me.

We were the quintessential Indian household and watching movies was a family passion. Along with our uncles and elder cousins we would go to the nearby Apsara and Minerva theatres or Lotus and Satyam in Worli. It was almost a crime to miss a Rajesh Khanna or an Amitabh Bachchan movie! In the evenings, our grandfather would give us lessons in Indian values and the entire thirteen-member gang would assemble around him. Once a year, we were required to read the whole *Ramayana* and occasionally visit the Hanuman Mandir in Lohar Chawl, none of which I particularly enjoyed.

From a fairly early age, I was completely against any religious practice or rituals and was quite open about it. The kid who had a perfect horoscope was soon turning into a black sheep of the family. I was always eager to get into an argument with my elders at the drop of a hat.

ANIL BIYANI*

Even as a kid, he used to act and behave differently, much to the annoyance of some family elders. His room was filled with posters of cars and cricket stars, but that was still okay. What really troubled others was his inclination to question every social or religious practice followed by the family. Someone had to give him a sound explanation before he would do anything religious.

A particular instance that I remember is that our family used to follow an old tradition of worshipping Sitala Devi (the Hindu Goddess who supposedly prevents the dreaded small pox disease). The ritual involved eating only cold food for a certain number of days. And here was Kishore who would refuse to follow such a diktat. His questioning was simple, 'If the school textbooks say that small pox has been fully eradicated, why still follow these rituals?'

Not only would he contradict every family member's wisdom, he revelled in being the devil's advocate as well. I still remember, while playing games as a kid he would say, 'You can be in Ram's team, and I will be in Ravan's

---

*Anil Biyani is Kishore's younger brother.

team and I am happy with that.' He trusted his own abilities so strongly from day one that he never needed to be on the side of an established hero.

We often played cricket by placing bets. He was ever willing to take up the opponent's challenge in spite of a weak team. Out of his own confidence he encouraged his team members to give it their best, even if they were destined to lose the match. And then, he did everything to win it.

I guess, from the very beginning I was obsessed with rationality. To make me do something, someone had to give me a very good reason or offer some amount of logic. Maybe I had read somewhere that human beings are rational and that stuck on, so I never had qualms in breaking dogmatic rules. In fact, I liked being a rebel in an extremely traditional family.

Looking back, I think that as someone grows and starts to learn and understand life, he starts to question as well. At a very early stage, one starts creating mental models to interpret various observations. At that point, if one finds that what he has learnt on his own is different from what is being practised in reality, he tries to distinguish the right from the wrong. He soon starts to seek answers to everything and then life transforms. I feel that having an attitude of questioning everything is very important. Until one questions the established way of doing things, one won't be able to come up with something new.

I don't know whether my family was different or not, but we made it change. I believe it was our generation and myself who were responsible for making the family look at things differently: first about the social customs that were being practised and some years later, the way it did business.

II

After finishing school, I joined H.R. College in Mumbai. All of a sudden I was exposed to a whole new world, far from the confines of Jeevan Vihar. I realised that growing up in a Malabar Hill locality didn't give me the real taste of life. In the midst of a thousand students, I was forced to look at things in a completely different way. It was quite a diverse class and we formed a fairly large group of friends, all from varied backgrounds. My days in college were probably the best learning phase of my student life. I learned about human dynamics, developed relationships and discovered life in general.

No, girls were quite scarce at our college and for a long time to come, I would be quite hesitant about interacting with them. The closest I came to a relationship during my days in college was with a girl who lived twelve hundred kilometres away in Kolkata — a pen-friend who I always wanted to meet but haven't managed to till date!

Attendance at college wasn't as serious an issue as it is made out to be today. I spent the better part of the day outside college with friends, wandering around new places and understanding and interpreting the real world. The evenings were spent at a small room located on the ground floor of Jeevan Vihar, next to the garage. We used to call it 'the den.' I guess, by then my family had realised that it was better to leave me alone and had furnished a room with a cot and some tables. Later an air cooler and a telephone were also added. Four close friends would meet there and discuss everything under the sun — movies, music, cricket, current affairs and sometimes business as well.

HEMANT BHOTIKA*

I met him while in queue at the admission counter of H.R. College. He seemed to be a very shy boy and like most of us, he was completely lost in the new environment. But that wasn't for long. Our favourite hangouts used to be the nearby food joints, and soon we were spending less time inside the classroom and more time outside it. When we had exhausted all our money eating at these restaurants, we gathered around the bonnets of the cars parked outside the college gate. Occasionally we would visit Oberoi's Samarkand restaurant.

The reason why I liked to visit Oberoi Hotel was because I came to know that Dhirubhai Ambani came to the hotel's health club almost every other day. Even if I could get a glimpse of him, I would be overjoyed. Reliance in the early Eighties had established itself strongly. I was quite fascinated by the company and its growth. I started reading about business during my college days and Dhirubhai Ambani was my first mental mentor, my personal role model. Maybe he was one of the few businessmen I could relate to. I discovered that Dhirubhai came from a very modest background. The fact that he had still managed to reach the pinnacle purely based on his own abilities was very inspiring. Most of the other big names in business at that time were men who had inherited it from their fathers or grandfathers. To me Dhirubhai

---

*Hemant Bhotika was a batch mate of Kishore in college and has been a close friend since then.

was a living proof of my belief that irrespective of one's background, it was possible to scale the heights of success.

I chose to study commerce in college probably because I felt that my skills in mathematics were very limited. I had known from early on that studying science wasn't my cup of tea. But I was willing to learn completely unrelated things that often surprised my batch mates. I learnt typing, did a course in import and export of garments and joined a programme run by the silk manufacturers' association, Sasmira. At one point, I almost decided to become a chartered accountant and even cleared the preliminary exams. But then I figured that CA coursework was too specialised and not meant for me. Rather than a specialist, I wanted to be a generalist — a jack-of-all-trades and master of some.

SANJAY SEKSARIA*

Kishore never had a mentor as such. But the thought of starting his own business was there in his mind probably from the second year in college. He was clear that he didn't want to join the family business. He would talk about getting into the garment trade and doing something very different. He obviously hadn't dreamed of what he is today, but he definitely had a big picture in mind. He was a keen observer and a very good judge of human beings. Even in college he would judge people and associate or disassociate himself from them accordingly. He wasn't

*Sanjay Seksaria and Kishore were in the same class at college. Sanjay is now married to Kishore's cousin, Kiran and is also a close business associate.

particularly vocal about it, but he made it clear that he didn't like loud people. But basically, he was an introvert and shy by nature.

The attitude to challenge everything was evident even in those days. At that time a retail outlet in Mumbai, Chiragh Din, was the most popular shop to buy shirts from. They would sell a large number of shirts every month and he would say, 'What's thirty thousand? I can do better.' He was always very self-assured even in college.

Chiragh Din was a fairly successful store at that time and once in a while I surveyed their store, what they stocked, their advertisements, promotions, etc. Advertising and marketing as subjects always fascinated me. I keenly studied advertisements, attended marketing seminars and for a year did a course in the latter as well.

My first brush with retailing was when as a teenager I visited Century Bazaar in Central Mumbai. It was bigger and brighter than what it is today. It had low ceilings that made it seem crowded and everything was sold over the counter, from vinyl records to apparels. The sheer size of the place and variety of merchandise got etched in my mind. It was probably then that I decided to create something similar or even better than this.

In college, we got together to form a social club and named it Kshitij. We used to screen movies or organise small festivals under the club's banner and the name struck a chord with me. Kshitij means horizon in Hindi and today our retail real estate fund has the same name.

However, the high point of my adolescent days was that of organising a disco *dandiya* festival at Jeevan Vihar. Disco *dandiya* is now very popular across Mumbai and beyond, but I can safely claim that the one at Jeevan Vihar in 1979 was the first of its kind in south Mumbai.

III

Dandiya, held during the festival of Dussehra, is a traditional Gujarati dance form. Young girls and boys dance in groups to the sound of folk music, and whirl around in circles within a set area. We used to have a *dandiya* festival in our housing compound as well, but it was extremely monotonous and boring.

Rajesh Roshan, at that time was my favourite music composer. His music band used to play live music at a *dandiya* festival in Juhu. In the first year of college, one of my friends took me there and I was completely taken aback by the scale of the event. There were more young people at one place than I had ever seen, and they were dancing to live Bollywood music being played by the band. The entire atmosphere was quite electric and we had an amazing time.

Then and there I started wondering why couldn't we replicate this at our locality next year and make it an even bigger event. A few months before Dussehra, I got together some of my college friends, my cousins and some other boys from the locality and explained the whole idea to them. Not all were convinced. Some wondered whether converting a traditional festival into a disco-like event would work. I was sure that it would, and decided to go ahead with it.

We hired strobe lights and signal lights to create a lighting effect similar to ones at the new discs coming up in the town. A music band that had played in some Hindi films was hired to belt out the latest Hindi movie numbers. Synthesisers and other electronic musical instruments replaced recorded folk music and that added to the whole novelty value. I was quite sure that the event had to be bigger and quite different from what was going on till then. These were the late Seventies and all these events weren't really common even in Mumbai. The invite to the event was called 'Passport,' suggesting that it would be an experience no teenager could afford to miss. I was even able to rope in a couple of advertisers, mostly by coaxing some uncles living in the same locality. They paid for the banners and that took care of the costs. When the day arrived, we were all taken aback by the turnout. Crowd management, though we hadn't heard of the term as yet, was the major issue at hand.

KIRAN SEKSARIA*

Kishore was the main organiser and we were the support pillars. What we saw on that day was absolutely stunning. More than five hundred people, some even from the suburbs had come over in the last few days of the event. There was gate-crashing and we had a hard time managing the crowd. But in those days there used to be hardly any eve-teasing or ugly behaviour.

Disco *dandiya* in the suburbs too was a recent phenomenon, having started only a year or two back. Soon Jeevan Vihar got a reputation for its disco *dandiya* festival and the word spread fast. Over the next few years more housing

---

*Kiran Seksaria is Kishore's first cousin.

complexes and localities in south Mumbai started organising their own disco *dandiya* festivals.

The whole event, a roaring success, was much beyond what we had expected. We continued to organise it for the next couple of years. It tested my organisational skills to the extreme and I was quite satisfied with the way we had managed to bring in advertisers and sponsors.

Looking back, I think this was the first popular trend that I picked on early and was able to capitalise on it. The event had struck a chord with many youngsters and I was an instant celebrity within the residential area and my entire friend circle. Most importantly, it gave a boost to my confidence in my ideas and abilities.

IV

Towards the final year in college, I started visiting our office in Kalbadevi. I spent some time working with my father, his five brothers and two elder cousins who had already joined the family trade. Bansi Silk Mills had set up its first manufacturing unit in Andheri in 1972 and a second unit had been set up in Parbatsar near Kishangarh, Ajmer. But I felt neither of them had the potential to grow beyond their existing size. The business was focussed primarily on trading in various kinds of fabrics. The company acted as an intermediary between the textile mills in Mumbai and the garment manufacturers. Margins were low and there was hardly any scope for growth. After I had pointed out all this to them, I was given the job of typing letters for official correspondence.

While still in college, I had decided that I wasn't going to continue in the family trade. I saw little reason in becoming the ninth member of the family to get involved in the same old routine. I realised I was not made to work in this kind of a business. Rather than seeking out new opportunities, they all seemed to be more inclined towards preserving the business the way it was. I trusted my own nose for business and felt the need to break away from it and start something on my own.

What I also found very disagreeable in the business was the obsession with financial control. The business was following a modified version of *parta*, a traditional form of accounting practised mostly by the Marwari community in India. In my opinion it was a regressive practice and I disliked it from day one. The *parta* system allows one to micro-manage, but it doesn't help one to grow the business. And if there are only accountants in each part of the business, where are the entrepreneurs going to come from?

LAXMINARAYAN BIYANI*

Kishore would come to office and within two or three hours, he would be irritated and leave. He neither liked our attitude, nor our approach towards the business. While he wouldn't confront us directly, it showed on his face. He would ask, 'Is this a business at all?' It was a trading business and we all were aware that the margins were too low to sustain. He suggested that we should set up large manufacturing facilities, but we didn't want to take large risks and were obviously quite hesitant about it.

*Laxminarayan Biyani is Kishore's father.

In the meantime, at college I noticed one of my more fashion-conscious friends wearing trousers made out of a new kind of fabric. He called it 'stonewash' fabric. It seemed fashionable simply because it was different and that somehow struck me. I borrowed it from him and showed it to some people I knew in the garment trade. A few weeks later I approached Jupiter Mills, one of the larger government-owned textile mills located in Mumbai. Some friend had suggested that they were planning to make stonewash fabric and I placed an order for two hundred metres of the cloth. Then, I tried selling these to a few garment manufacturers and a few small shops in the city.

Some other traders too had started introducing this fabric in the Mumbai market and much to my surprise it became quite popular among the trendy college-going crowd. In the next six months I was able to sell a few lakhs of rupees worth of stonewash fabric. That's how I made my first profit. By now I was fully convinced that I could chart my own entrepreneurial course.

In the meantime, my parents had introduced me to Sangita Rathi. After a six months' courtship, we got married in November 1983. But as the day of marriage came closer, I remember throwing some tantrums about the elaborate ceremonies that were being planned. I also didn't like the over-decorated *sherwani* that I was supposed to wear on the day of the marriage. Though we sell them in large numbers, I have never been particularly fond of Indian ethnic wear myself. On the day of the marriage, my friend Sanjay had to rush and get a regular, clean white *sherwani*. That too, I wore grudgingly.

Ever since, in the last twenty-three years, Sangita has lived with the maximum share of such tantrums. And yet, over the years, she has reinforced my self-belief, and given me immense succour and courage. She has taken my erratic schedules in her stride as well as what my friends call my 'finicky' nature.

SANGITA BIYANI*

His reputation of being a rebel preceded him. Even before I met him, many people cautioned me that he had a different outlook towards everything in life. We met each other and were engaged in two days.

I somehow found him interesting and good to talk to. And frankly, I didn't care about anything else. I didn't want my husband to be traditional, or like some of the regular Marwari boys who used to wear strange rings or funny dresses. I had grown up in an open environment and he suited me perfectly well. He wasn't in the habit of showing off and whenever we met, he was just himself...

But before marriage, he did warn me that he was very different from all his relations and he may move out of the joint family structure. He wanted to do everything on his own. He didn't look for or expect support from any of his family members.

Even during the wedding ceremony, he had to be forced to perform all the customs and rituals. Right from the beginning, he didn't pay much heed to advice from family members, only because they were family. In any case, few in the family could really grasp or make sense of him and his thought process.

---

*Sangita Biyani is Kishore's wife.

They all had merely resigned themselves to the fact that he was different. But no one really expected anything grand or spectacular from him. However the one positive thing was that while my father-in-law did not encourage him to pursue his own ideas, he did not prevent him from doing things on his own either.

And hence started my entrepreneurial journey.

V

There are three kinds of entrepreneurs — creators, preservers and destroyers. My father and uncles, much like most other entrepreneurs in India, were preservers. I consider myself to be both creator and destroyer. Preserving the status quo has never been my cup of tea. A continuous process of change and of growth has to be there in every business. If a business doesn't grow and evolve, it is not an enterprise at all.

India has probably the highest number of entrepreneurs in the world. All of us know that there is a lot of latent entrepreneurial talent in our country. Just throwing a glance around, we would find lots of local and regional entrepreneurs across the country. And there are people who have built very successful businesses here. But the majority of them are limited in scale or geography. Somehow, despite being such a big nation, we always think small and often lack the initiative to grow beyond a certain size.

The primary reason behind this, I think, is that our family system works against entrepreneurship. Parents discourage their children from taking large risks or getting into uncertain territory. They constrict their vision and the ability to think expansively.

From my own experience, my family reluctantly agreed to what I chose to do, but never encouraged any of us to think beyond our means. They were quite conservative and I have found this kind of limitation even among other so-called business communities of India — the Gujaratis, Parsis, Chettiars, etc.

By the time one manages to get out of the control of one's family, one loses his zeal and becomes complacent with what has already been created. Instead of growing the business, he gets into the mode of preserving it. He just stops short of taking any risk. But taking chances and going against the conventional approach are necessary grounds for the growth of any business.

Business, as I realised soon after my college days, is a lot like multiple-choice questions. One has to guess and select one of the three options and just trust it to be the right one. Even if one has a one-third chance of being successful, it's good enough to put in all the effort and make it happen.

I did not have a mentor and most successful entrepreneurs don't necessarily have the luxury of having one. I created my own 'mental' mentors, studied various subjects and eagerly sought knowledge. I strongly believe that there is a hard and arduous journey that one has to undertake alone. I was lucky that I understood very early on that I had to do everything on my own and that no one was going to help.

Lot of people blame others when they fail. Someone else has to be blamed and if they can't find any particular person, they blame it on God. I believe that as an entrepreneur, I have to take responsibility for what I have done and created. I can't hide behind the excuse that someone else didn't deliver or the external environment wasn't good enough for me to grow. No one ever promised that in business one gets a level-playing field. So, whenever something misfired, I faced my mistakes, learned from them and moved ahead. And I always felt there might be a hidden opportunity waiting to be captured in each challenge I encountered.

Entrepreneurship is about thinking big, believing in your own ability and going ahead with huge risks even if you are aware that some of the ventures may not be successful. It's also about making decisions, leadership, and about making your colleagues believe in your dream.

Building an enterprise is a dream, a vision, and in my case it kept growing every time I reached a new milestone. The one crucial thing that helped me was my ability to think in terms of a mass customer base and focus on a single-minded pursuit of growth.

I just couldn't think anything elitist. I have never understood people who spend a few lakhs on a pen or a watch. None of my businesses will ever cater to them. Instead, my biggest fear is getting into a situation where I lose touch with the public. I am almost paranoid about it. Our business is entirely dependent on observing people, understanding their emotions and catering to their needs; it has been our imperative as a mass player.

Each of these attributes were lacking in our family business. To put things in the correct perspective, it was not unique. Like most other businesses in India, it too suffered from the 'preserver' syndrome. And I knew that only by breaking away from this mindset could I become a true entrepreneur.

Having said that, there was one thing that I found worth learning from our family business. At our shop in Kalbadevi, we would sit on *gaddis* — thick mattresses supported by round pillows. One still finds them in the old business districts like Kalbadevi in Mumbai, or Burra Bazaar in Kolkata. Well, it wasn't just the *gaddis* that I liked; I admired the basic structure of the setup. The *seth* or the owner squatted on the *gaddi* in a corner and was surrounded by the *munim* (chief accountant) and his deputies. The deputies could talk directly with the *seth* whenever they wanted, accounts were written without vouchers on the statements itself and the *seth* could directly interact with his clients and customers.

This ensured a direct flow of information, insights and knowledge from the customer front. Modern-day businesses are structured in a way that most of the critical details of the ground level are lost in the multiple layers of the organisation. We make grand presentations and have long meetings just to share data. Often, the only outcome of these meetings is deciding when to meet next. By the time the data reaches the top, it's either been misinterpreted or has become irrelevant.

Existing organisational structures were designed during the industrial age. We may talk about knowledge economy but the overall organisational structures aren't very different from those of the yesteryears. In this era, ideas are the biggest assets for any company. Organisations that allow insights and information to flow freely will be the ones to come up with the best ideas. Significant de-layering and creating a seamless organisation is the only route to success.

As of now, we have five layers or bands within our company and I don't see any reason why we can't do with just three — the information gathering layer, the knowledge creation layer and the strategy layer. Reducing to just two layers like the *seth's* may not be possible, but an organisation with three layers can be created. Thus, building a completely seamless organisation is going to be one of my primary objectives over the next ten years.

Defying the Odds

✡

'The unlimited power that lies sleeping
within you, let it slumber no more.'

ANTHONY ROBINS

I

With the success of stonewash fabric I had tasted blood. I started to desperately look around for something new. A few of my elder cousins by that time had started their own trades. These were mostly around plastics, corrugated paperboards and packaging. I worked with them for some time but it could not sustain my interest. It was good to learn about new businesses, but none of these had the mass appeal I was looking for. I wanted to try out something that would reach out to maximum number of people in the country.

Over the next fifteen years, I kept looking for a beachhead to realise my dream. It was the early Eighties and there was a distinct sense of optimism. The young and energetic Prime Minister Rajiv Gandhi was in many ways ushering in the first wave of liberalisation. I felt that this was the time to try different things, new things. I started looking around for big ideas that could be ideal for the 'new' India that was emerging.

Much to the displeasure of my family and well-wishers, I got my hands dirty in multiple businesses all at the same time. Some of these businesses were moderately successful but most of them had to be closed down after a few years. However, in some way or the other, each of these businesses contributed to my understanding of customers and formed the foundation of what is today our company.

One of the first things I got involved in was launching a brand of fabric for men's trousers. I named it WBB. It was a simple abbreviation of the three most popular colours for trousers those days — White, Blue and Brown. Yet, it was smart, catchy and unique. Come to think of it, what else does one need?

I would visit small textile mills around the city and buy fabrics that I liked. Then I would try to sell these to garment manufacturers and shop owners in the Kalbadevi area. Readymade garments hadn't really become popular till that time. People bought fabric and got it stitched at a tailor's shop. The major fabric brands used to be Vimal, Raymond and Bombay Dyeing but some small brands like Cliff, Double Bull, UFO, and Buffalo were also there, that sold trousers.

There was a particular gentleman whom we used to call Ahmedbhai. He was the owner of the Cliff brand. His office was in the Shah and Nahar Industrial Estate in Lower Parel. For months I would drop in at his office and spend hours waiting, before he called me in. It was a frustrating experience. That was the time I promised myself that no one would have to wait outside my office and waste his time.

I also used to regularly set up my own stall at various textile exhibitions and fairs across the city. Apart from getting in touch with potential customers, it was a good way to keep a check on what others in the industry were up to. These fairs were usually hosted at large hotels. But often I didn't have the money to pay for the high fees. I would then rent a small hall or a shop just outside the hotel and wait for people visiting the fair inside to drop by on their way.

Those were truly trying times. But I was fortunate enough to have the unstinted support of two family members. My wife, Sangita came with me to these exhibitions and that was huge encouragement. And my younger brother, Anil too started helping me in whatever I was doing. Anil in all ways fits into the classical definition of the younger brother. He has full faith in my abilities and never hesitated to join me whenever I needed his help.

Another person, who has worked with me since I started, is Raju. He used to help us in packing and carrying our boxes and till date he continues to be my man Friday.

ANIL BIYANI*

Around this time, Kishore did three dramatic things. The first was naming the brand WBB. The traditional way was to name a product after the name of a god or a family member, like Mahavir Saris or Bansi Silk. But he had no intentions of that nature. He believed that the brand should relate to the products.

Then, he went ahead and decided to spend a few lakh rupees on advertising; again something that most felt was foolhardy. He even hired an advertising agency for it. My uncles would often speak to my father and point out how even before he had showed any results, he had drawn up an expenditure plan that was scary.

However, it was the third step that really took everyone by surprise. The family had 600 square metres of land in an industrial area in Andheri, a northern suburb of Mumbai. Kishore had taken the initiative of constructing a two-storeyed building and we were planning to set up a couple of looms over there. One fine sunny morning, he went to the Kalbadevi office, picked up a typewriter, a chair and a table, hired a tempo and along with Raju left for the Andheri office. At that time, it was almost taboo for us living in Malabar Hills to travel twenty-five kilometres to

---

*Anil Biyani is Kishore's younger brother.

far away Andheri for work. By now, everyone was convinced that he had gone crazy.

I think we did a fairly good job of establishing the WBB brand. At its peak, we sold thirty to forty thousand metres of branded fabric every month. At times I would spend time at the loom to get some job-work done on the fabric.

The power of branding also became evident with the success of WBB. The next step was how could we take the brand ahead, add some more value to our products and start to compete against the big boys in the business.

ABHAY KUMAT*

I first got in touch with Kishore during the mid-Eighties, when I was working for Pashupati Spinning. He came over to our office and showed some of his WBB products. I asked him what the brand meant. His reply was, 'It is innovative.' I thought he was crazy.

Whenever I would meet him henceforth, he would be carrying these fashion forecast brochures, shade cards and style files with him and would enthusiastically show them to us. I still don't know where he used to get these foreign brochures from, but he had stacks of them. One day he turned up at our office and showed us one Italian fashion forecast book. It had a complete collection of trouser fabrics in various shades. They were mostly made from

---

*Abhay Kumat is a long-standing friend of Kishore. He is involved in the textile business.

trilobal polyesters that gave the fabric a distinct shine. After my boss and I went through the book, Kishore said that we should get the entire range of yarns. I introduced him to Raju Amaarnani of Harry's Collection, who had a fabric manufacturing facility in Mumbai. In association with Amaarnani we created a special collection of fabrics — and introduced checks in trouser designs — that was probably among the first of its kind in the country.

Abhay Kumat went on to become my friend and also one of my biggest critics. With the short success of WBB, I thought it was a good idea to go one step ahead and start selling readymade men's trousers. I got around thirty to forty trousers stitched at Andheri and showed it to some shop owners. But none of them seemed interested in doing business with a small company like ours. By the end of 1985, with the help of another friend I set up a 400 square feet shop at C.P. Tank near Bombay Central railway terminus. It sold men's trousers and we called it Patloon. That was my first retail experience.

SANGITA BIYANI*

For Kishore, Patloon was more of an experiment. He would go to the shop in the afternoon, come back all excited and spend the whole evening telling me how two or three trousers got sold that day. Selling readymade garments didn't make sense during those days and no one took him seriously. Even family members used to find it

---

*Sangita Biyani is Kishore's wife.

funny. Often people would come up to me and say, 'We
are not tailors. Why is he doing the tailor's job?' Fed up
with such remarks I would often nudge him and all he
would say is, *'kya farak parta hai?'* (What difference does
it make?). He was least bothered about what others said
as long as he was confident about his plans. Soon I too
started discarding such remarks.

II

Around the time I was setting up the office at Andheri, my family
had acquired some land in another industrial park being developed
by Maharashtra Industrial Development Corporation (MIDC) in
Tarapur. It is located around a hundred kilometres north of Mumbai
and was already home to a number of textile and petroleum-based
factories. My uncles wanted to set up a processing unit over there,
but I felt that the land was not suitable for that. I had come across
some fabric with fancy fibres at a shop in the Paidhuni area in
Mumbai. It turned out to be imported material and I felt that
developing similar yarns that gave different textures to fabrics
might be a good prospect. It was a high value-add business and
my gut feel was that the use of these yarns could set a new fashion
trend. The raw material being used for these was filament yarn
that was already being manufactured in India by companies like
Century Enka and Reliance Petroleum. One of my friends
introduced me to Krishna Jhunjhunwala who was a distributor for
textile products made by Reliance and a couple of the mills owned
by National Textile Corporation.

I started exploring the business opportunity of how we could
make these with Krishna. We figured that we both had rudimentary

knowledge about textiles manufacturing, so we needed help from someone who had been in the industry for a long time. We got in touch with Sushil Sain who was then the chairman of National Textile Mills, South Maharashtra; that owned thirty-five textile mills across the state, including in Mumbai. Krishna used to deal with him once in a while. It was early 1985 and he was about to retire from the company the next year. Krishna met him, discussed the things we had in mind and asked if he would like to be our partner. He seemed to be the ideal person but I wasn't sure whether someone of his stature would like to partner with a bunch of twenty-somethings trying to set up a small plant. When I met him for the first time at his house in Bandra, it was with a mild sense of trepidation.

SUSHIL SAIN*

My first impression of Kishore was of a young, timid, but honest boy. He had already briefed Krishna on what he was looking for and hardly spoke himself. But when he finally did, he made lot of sense. He had a very clear vision of what he wanted to do, a good understanding of textiles and was up to date with all the market information. The initial vibes were very positive.

However, having been associated with large corporations throughout my career, it was difficult for me to imagine that I would be involved in such a small venture. But Kishore had done his homework well. The business plans

*Sushil Sain is among the founder-members on the board of Directors of Pantaloon Retail.

and the profitability figures on paper looked quite genuine and exciting.

In retrospect, I find that he had visualised this as an opportunity much before anyone else had. Probably the same is true for his success in retail. Neither money nor success has transformed him. He still has the same simplicity. He has done a fantastic job but what's more important is that he is a wonderful person.

The fact that a person of the standing and calibre of Sushil Sain was willing to mentor us at that stage, just goes on to prove that if one's determination and intent is right, nothing is too difficult to achieve. A crucial lesson I learnt from Sushil Sain was the importance of making quick decisions. He taught me how to make decisions and execute them well. He was my mentor for some time to come and we still maintain a very close relationship.

We started working on setting up a small fancy-yarn plant at Tarapur. That time one had to travel by train to a station called Boisar and then take a *tonga* ride (cart pulled by mules) to reach Tarapur. The three of us invested Rs 3 lakh each in the company. The company was named Dhruv Synthetics and we commissioned the factory in mid-1986. The machines came from Coimbatore and they were fitted with microprocessors that gave the fabric an effect of fancy yarn. We started off with four machines and soon with the profits that were generated, we were able to increase the number of machines to twelve. Each of the machines could make around fifty kilograms of fancy yarn every day.

That year all of us went to Paris to visit the International Textile Machinery Exposition, which is held once every four

years. It was my first visit abroad. On the way, I stopped over
at London and went to check out the Marks & Spencer outlet.
Many years back, as a youngster, I had thought Century Bazaar
in Mumbai to be the biggest shop possible. Visiting the Marks
& Spencer store in London was a big eye-opener. I had heard
about it, read about it but never seen anything of this kind before.
This new image of a gorgeous, king-sized shop got stuck in my
mind. More than a decade later, when we opened Pantaloons in
Kolkata, someone walked up to me and said that it seemed like
the Marks & Spencer of India. That was probably the best
compliment I could have got at the time.

During the first year of operation, we did some pretty good
numbers. We sold goods worth almost a crore of rupees and
earned a neat profit. People were becoming more fashion conscious
and we used to get large orders from fashion designers and even
exporters. Plans were afoot to expand the business further. But
things don't always go the way you want them to.

Tarapur, at that time, was notorious for labour disputes. We
were aware of it, but somehow felt that a small factory like ours
wouldn't get affected. But some of the nearby factories were
already facing severe problems and it wasn't long before the
labour unions made their presence felt at our company as well.
We tried to address some of the genuine problems; for instance
we acquired land to develop housing facilities for our workers.
Somehow the labour leader of the area wasn't really in a mood
to resolve the trouble. Orders started piling up but due to frequent
strikes we couldn't deliver on them. We tried to control the
production process but the union leader came up with new demands
every time we got to the negotiating table. Finally, we had little
option but to shut down the facility.

The shutdown came as a nasty jolt to me. But thankfully, during that time I had also taken up the distributorship of denims made by Arvind Mills.

In the Eighties, denims were becoming quite popular in the market. And most of the demand was being catered to by imports. Arvind Mills was on its way to set up the largest denim factory in the world and capture the huge domestic market. I spotted this opportunity and got very passionate about it. Every Wednesday I would take the overnight Saurashtra Express to go to Ahmedabad, meet people there and place orders at the Arvind Mills office. Rest of the week was spent setting up a network of salesmen to sell the denims at large apparel stores. With the advent of denims, readymade men's wear was finally being accepted in India and we had already been planning a major foray into the manufacture and distributorship of these. While Dhruv Synthetics had a very brief history, the experience of managing a manufacturing facility gave me the toehold to take an even larger leap.

III

Manz Wear Private Limited was incorporated on 12th of October 1987. I was a little over twenty-six years old and my last five years had been spent understanding the textile industry. We started off as a garment manufacturer, launched a couple of brands, got into franchising and direct marketing and ten years later plunged into modern retail. During this time, the company's name changed from Manz Wear to Pantaloon Fashion and subsequently to Pantaloon Retail, reflecting the changing nature of the business.

The company was founded with a seed capital of Rs 7 lakh and an initial production capacity to make two hundred trousers per day. The trousers were sold under the brand name of Pantaloon. I am not sure what inspired me to choose this brand name; probably it was a heavy dose of the Italian fashion magazines that I used to buy often. It almost sounded like the Urdu word for trousers, *patloon*, yet had a trendy feel to it.

Within a year of its operation, the company touched a turnover of Rs 32 lakh. But it also registered a loss of Rs 8 lakh. The main reason for that of course was the Rs 16 lakh we spent on advertising and brand building alone.

For me the amazing thing was being witness to a revolution. Earlier people dealt with 'fabrics;' in the new era, it was called 'fashion.' The change of a single word implied a new meaning and a metamorphosis in the very concept of clothing. People were becoming fashion conscious and dressing up was in. Instead of going to tailors, they started buying from readymade garment stores. I was bent upon garnering a decent share in this emerging space.

Marketing, advertising and the power of branding had always held a deep attraction for me. I feel an advertisement captures the people behind the brand, their way of thinking and what has gone into the making of the brand. I studied advertisements very closely and interpreted organisations based on the ads they carried. I wanted to position our company as a fashion house and we spent heavily in creating a major communications campaign for our brand.

For the next few years, we continued to invest disproportionately large sums of money into building our brands, even when it hurt our bottom line. The branded apparel segment was extremely fragmented and I think with the help of our ad agency we did a fairly good job of establishing our trouser brand, Pantaloon.

SAMEER SAIN*

During one of my summer vacations, my father sent me to work at Kishore's Andheri workshop. At that time, I remember, there was a tailor who would give final touches to the trousers and my job was to fold these trousers, pack and mark them, and then load them in the back of taxis. It was very much a start-up environment and I would do this along with one of Kishore's younger cousins, Ghanshyam. Kishore also folded the trousers, sealed the boxes, typed the invoices, signed the cheques and pretty much did everything.

Kishore used to be very creative with his designs and maybe the designs were a bit ahead of the times. A particular one, which I remember, had three buttons above the zipper and a very high waist. It was unconventional but not gaudy. I started wearing those Pantaloon trousers, and I remember them becoming quite popular with my friends.

Kishore sounded quite ambitious and I was so convinced about it that I used to tell my father to take a franchise of Pantaloon. He sparked off a lot of entrepreneurial instinct in me at that time.

Towards the end of the first financial year, we moved back to Tarapur to a new and larger facility. I was looking for new technology

---

*Sameer Sain is the son of Sushil Sain, Kishore's Partner in Dhruv Synthetics. In December 2005 he quit his job as Managing Director at Goldman Sach (Europe) to become a Partner and MD of Future Capital Holdings.

that could significantly boost production. At a textile machinery exhibition in Mumbai I came across imported, automatic Donear weaving machines. They were expensive and we borrowed some money from a bank to set these up at the Tarapur plant. The advanced technology helped us increase production and we started looking at how we could expand further.

ANIL BIYANI*

Kamlesh Merchant used to work with us as a technical consultant and machinery indenting agent. He was aware that Kishore was looking for more advanced weaving machines. On a trip to Germany, he came across a distributor for these machines who was willing to sell twenty-four weaving machines of the latest technology. He called up Kishore and asked him to fly down to Germany, take a first hand look at these machines and negotiate the prices. But Kishore didn't think twice and asked him to immediately place an order. He told Kamlesh that since his own understanding of technology was far less than that of Kamlesh it was better that he closed the deal as early as possible. Till date, whenever I meet Kamlesh, he reminds me of this incident. 'How can a person strike such a huge deal on the phone?' he wonders. A big picture with a hundred such machines was running in Kishore's mind and a few lakh rupees that we could have saved from bargaining really didn't bother him.

---

*Anil Biyani is Kishore's younger brother.

The big picture was definitely becoming clearer to me. Though the profit margins in the business were still razor-thin, I was looking forward to scaling up the business significantly. During this time, we were basically supplying to some apparel outlets in Mumbai and some other places. Good amount of investments had already been made into building the Pantaloon brand and I was looking at how we could leverage its increasing popularity.

However, the biggest stumbling block turned out to be distribution and the capital needed to set up a decent network. We were trying to sell these trousers to various shops in and around Mumbai and it wasn't really an easy job. A friend had opened an apparel store in Goa which was not faring well. I suggested to him that we could set up a Pantaloon franchise shop that would sell only our trousers. A franchisee network seemed to be an ideal way of ramping up our reach across the country. He willingly agreed to it and our first franchise store opened in Goa in 1991. It was called Pantaloon Shoppe.

Once the Pantaloon Shoppe in Goa opened, I wanted to set a nation-wide franchisee network. The next set of Pantaloon Shoppes came up in Cochin and Ernakulam in Kerela, Colaba and Andheri in Mumbai, on Ahmedabad's C.G. Road and at Chennai's T. Nagar.

The denim distribution business with Arvind Mills had by then grown to a significant size and was adding to our revenues substantially. Yet, it also meant that we were essentially trading in somebody else's brand and making small margins on it. Now that we had understood and developed the denim market to some extent, we decided to launch our own jeans brand, Bare Necessities.

Next came the idea to make Pantaloon Shoppe a one-stop destination for all apparel products for men — shirts, trousers, sports and denim wear, socks, ties and handkerchiefs. A brand of shirts was launched under the name Knighthood and we also introduced handkerchiefs, ties and socks under this name. With this, the Pantaloon Shoppe got positioned as a complete men's wear destination. By the end of 1991, there were twenty-two of them across the country. Most of these were small shops located in popular shopping areas.

By 1991, the production capacity at Tarapur had grown significantly and we were also outsourcing some manufacturing to other factories. But expanding the franchisee network and distributing the products demanded a lot of investment, and none of us had the funds to do that. Low margins and internal accruals, due to high promotional and operational costs meant that we had to raise capital from external sources to fund our growth plans.

The textile industry in and around Mumbai was facing a lot of challenges. Frequent strikes in the previous decade, coupled with increasing costs had brought the industry to its knees. Interest rates were way too high and no banker worth his salt was willing to take an exposure in this sector.

The only way to raise funds was by approaching the stock market. The liberalisation policy brought in by the new government in 1991 had boosted the stock markets. Not only was the Sensex on a high, the primary market was seeing an unprecedented amount of activity.

In May 1992, we announced an initial public offer (IPO) at the Mumbai, Delhi and Ahmedabad stock exchanges to raise Rs 225 lakh.

IV

During the initial public offer, we diluted sixty percent of our holding to raise Rs 225 lakh. The public offer made at the par value of Rs 10 sailed through and provided for a substantial chunk of money we needed. However, everything comes at a price and going public meant that we were not only answerable to a large number of shareholders, but also our operations and performance were available for scrutiny by competitors and business associates. For a start-up company, it wasn't easy to meet the investors' expectations each quarter.

Dalal Street obviously expected us to deliver profits at every stage of our growth. Maybe things would have been different if we hadn't focussed so much on our bottom line in the initial years. In fact, the amount of money we raised now seems to be small and we may have been far better off if we had waited a few years more and listed the company at a much higher valuation. But I don't have any regrets.

I always seized the opportunities that came my way. And raising money from the stock exchange was an opportunity I didn't want to let pass. There was a wave of excitement vis-à-vis the newly liberated economic environment at the time. Capital was a major constraint for us and a lot of entrepreneurs had begun to approach the primary markets in the early Nineties. And investors, on the other hand, were putting their stakes into every public offer being launched.

When one is young and tries to rewrite rules, he is called 'mad.' But when he is finally successful, because he dared to risk it, he is called a 'maverick.' Unable to understand why I was placing such huge bets, two of my uncles separated themselves from the business in 1997, just before we got into modern retail. Obviously, the stock market was even less understanding and accommodative of my ideas. Our share price languished for a long time, well after we launched the Pantaloons department store, touching an all time low of Rs 1.50 in November, 1998. Banks for long shied away from lending money because retail wasn't classified as a separate industry but clubbed with the textile sector.

I do believe that stock markets are the most efficient distributor of capital. Yet, it takes time for the stock market to judge companies and their real value. The markets ignored us for a fairly long time, but we were confident about what we were doing. We didn't allow the stock market performance to affect our business plans. We continued to experiment and learn on the way. Of course, poor valuation did pose serious difficulties to raising further capital, but then business isn't a cakewalk, and neither did we expect it to be one.

ABHAY KUMAT*

During the mid-Nineties, Pantaloon's vendors and suppliers used to have a tough time. While they were sure that the company wouldn't go belly-up, there were still plenty of issues that worried them. The chief among them was payments getting delayed by months on end.
Kishore was aware of these problems and he was concerned. But he was a man in a hurry. He just wouldn't get into financial details or allow them to affect the growth plans. To him the big picture was always important, no matter what the immediate concerns were. Whenever I met him, I would bring about this topic of the suppliers' payments getting delayed. All he would say was, 'Abhay, I am looking

---

*Abhay Kumat is a long-standing friend of Kishore. He is involved in the textile business.

at doing business worth Rs 100 crore in a few years. A problem involving a few thousand rupees is incidental.' He was disturbed and tense, but he would put up a strong face. He never allowed financial constraints to affect his vision and ambition.

Financial matters were important but we didn't want them to be the overarching factor in our decision-making process. I was quite determined that I wouldn't allow this company to be ruled by accountants. I had witnessed the stunted growth of many family businesses due to their obsession with financial control. So, like any other challenge, we approached these issues with some out-of-the-box thinking and found solutions to address them. The bottom line is, whenever we desperately needed funds, we were able to raise them.

I don't think any business plan can die just because of lack of funds. If one has a solid proposition and is willing to put all his effort into making it successful, he can find people willing to help him out. However, if funding is given primary importance, one will get stuck. Making finance the starting point of a decision-making process, stops businesses from taking many initiatives and ultimately slows down growth.

CHANDRA PRAKASH TOSHNIWAL*

Even during my interview, Kishoreji was very clear that financial and cost control wasn't exactly at the top of his

---

*Chandra Prakash Toshniwal is the Head of Corporate Planning at Pantaloon Retail. He joined the company in 1995.

priority list. For him, the finance and account function was critical only to the extent that it should provide him with accurate information that can help him make sound business decisions.

As accountants, we had been trained in the traditional style of financial control. And unlike many other companies of that era, the finance department at Pantaloon wasn't the most powerful one. Soon after I joined, it became clear to me that Kishoreji would never let financial control get in the way of his business. He always looked around for innovative ways for addressing financial constraints.

The circumstances were tough and there was a lot of pressure from investors to consolidate the business and focus on improving the bottom line. What they essentially wanted was to slow down the business and avoid taking too much risk. Instead, I focussed on how we could sustain growth and somehow also keep the investors' trust in us intact. Many steps we took were fairly exceptional and we were often the first in our industry to do it.

Everyone thought that our expenditure towards advertisement and publicity was way too high for a company our size. I suggested that the money spent on brand building be interpreted as investments that would give us benefits over the long-term. It was in keeping with my fundamental conviction that brands would one day become our greatest intangible assets. By 1993, we started to amortise the promotional expenses over four years.

We then asked an independent valuer to put a value to our brands. This practice had till then been limited to some pharmaceutical companies and had never been tried in the textile industry. We went ahead with it and arrived at a fair value for our brands, which was reflected on our balance sheet. Subsequently, we leveraged the estimated value of brands to raise large sums of money from private and public sector banks. There were other initiatives like securitising future credit card receivables that helped us raise more money and even prompted lenders to fund our growth plans.

During this time, something that could have completely changed our way of doing business was getting into exports. One of my friends had studied the apparel market in Europe and offered his help in testing the export market for our products. India had then recently joined the WTO and many textile companies started to focus exclusively on exports. We too tried our hand at it, exporting to Italy, the US and the Middle East. We even got very close to setting up a joint venture with a small UK based company to manufacture trousers in India and export them to Europe. I know now it was good that the project didn't materialise.

The export market was too fragmented and over-dependent on external factors. Changes in government regulations, both foreign and Indian, and quota agreements could have affected the business. I also felt that we wouldn't be able to reach the kind of scale I envisaged for our company if we concentrated on exports. Moreover, there was hardly any control on the business and little scope of developing our own brands in the foreign market. India was way too big an opportunity to miss out on and we decided that it was far better to concentrate on the Indian market and capitalise the potential over here.

I believe my strength lies in understanding the needs and aspirations of the Indian customer. The Indian customer both challenges and intrigues me and as an organisation we still do not completely understand each section of our population. Our focus has been and will continue to be on watching, evaluating and capitalising the domestic consumption space. It is such a vast and diverse market by itself that there seems no apparent need to venture outside in the next couple of decades.

V

From a fairly early stage, the guiding principle of our business had been, 'to provide the ordinary people what only the rich can afford.' To tap into the mass market, we knew we had to offer a very strong value-for-money proposition to our customers. Though we never communicated this overtly to our customers, all our brands were positioned in the low to middle price bracket.

Our range started from Rs 199 for white shirts and Rs 250 for black trousers. Pantaloon trousers were positioned as formal, executive trousers and it complemented the Knighthood brand of shirts. Bare was projected as a dynamic brand targeted at the young Indian. As branded denim wear, it was far cheaper than the expensive international labels that were flooding the market. We also forayed into a couple of niche markets with this brand. We were the first to introduce branded women's denim wear under this label. And it had a sub-brand called Mr. BIG that catered to plus-size male customers with waist sizes above forty. Bare also had a couple of exclusive franchisee outlets.

This was the period when a number of foreign apparel labels were launched in India and there was the seemingly profitable option to tie up with a foreign brand or to buy its franchise. Instead, we registered a shirts brand with a decidedly American name, John Miller. It went with the tagline, 'A shirt inspired by America,' and most customers thought it was a foreign brand. It was aggressively priced for the mass market, but projected as an 'aspirational' brand. The game plan worked just the way we had expected it to. John Miller became extremely popular and caught the fancy of customers. Both Bare and John Miller are now among the largest apparel brands in the country.

It was during this period that we first started to study the market very closely. India historically has been a savings-led society. Not only are we very value-conscious, nothing in this country is ever wasted or thrown away. Women in India are trained from their childhood to preserve everything. This holds true for apparels as well. The average Indian wears the same shirt or trouser for years, well after its colours have faded or the buttons have come off. In every Indian city there are women who trade new steel utensils for old clothes that are then sold in a second hand market. Many middle class housewives eagerly participate in this barter.

This has always posed one of the biggest challenges to marketers and retailers. To turn the customer in our direction, we started the first exchange programme for denims in the country. A certain discount on a new pair of jeans was offered in exchange for an old pair. It proved to be a whopping success.

Today, exchange programmes are common across all categories, be it apparels, cars or televisions. So we have now taken it to another level altogether and it is one of the most popular customer initiatives at Big Bazaar. Customers are encouraged to bring anything and everything that they don't use any longer. You may notice droves of customers lining up outside Big Bazaar and unloading old clothes, utensils, newspapers, bottles from cars and autos. These are weighed and coupons are issued at a fixed price for every kilogram of goods collected. Customers then use these coupons to pay for one-fourth of their total bill at Big Bazaar.

People often ask us what we do with all the old stuff. We merely sell them to scavengers and *raddiwalas*, but for us the exchange programme translates into higher spending at our store. For example, to redeem an exchange coupon of Rs 25 a customer has to purchase goods worth Rs 100. Customers love this offer because it effectively means that they get a twenty-five percent discount. And they spend much more at our store than they had initially planned for. This programme may have made us the biggest *raddiwalas* in the country, but it was also responsible for a sizeable portion of the annual sales at Big Bazaar last year.

Innovative promotions like these were quite common at all Pantaloon Shoppe outlets and we would have them throughout the year. When we noticed that some customers were still not comfortable buying readymade trousers, we launched Pantalength. It was a do-it-yourself kit for making trousers, complete with fabric, buttons and threads. We developed a direct-selling model for this product and hired close to two thousand young boys who would visit apartments and offices selling our products. It helped us reach out to new customers and increase the brand awareness, and it proved to be quite successful.

These ideas came essentially from observation and interacting with individuals from different professions. I used to travel a lot and meet up with unconventional people who could give me such ideas.

DARLIE O. KOSHY*

I first met Kishore during my days as a faculty member at National Institute of Fashion Technology in Delhi. I

---

*Dr Darlie O. Koshy is Director, National Institute of Design (NID), Ahmedabad. He is also a member of the board of Directors of Pantaloon Retail.

used to regularly write for some fashion magazines and Kishore must have read some of them. I met him through another young entrepreneur whom I knew and Kishore was supplying fabrics to him.

My first impression of him was that here is an entrepreneur who is so keen to know about fashion and retail. His focus was on selling fabric, but beyond that he saw the branding revolution coming. He was a small-time businessman but had an open mind and a determination to grow. He hadn't travelled overseas a great deal, but was a prolific observer — therefore well updated — and had a deep respect for creative people.

He would drop in at our institute from time to time to know more about fabric, about design and about how to build brands. He would observe the most innocuous things and discuss his vision and dreams passionately. He himself came from a rather middle-income business background and he understood the income disparities in India.

With brands like Pantaloon, Bare and John Miller, we started getting a lot of enquiries from across the country asking for the franchise for Pantaloon Shoppe. Choosing the right partners was always a tricky affair. More than financial muscle, it was important to understand the values of the person we were going to partner with. I remember having a two-step screening test. I would visit the store of prospective franchisees a little before they were scheduled to open. The first objective was to check whether the store opens on time. Then, immediately after the shutters were pulled up, I would walk into the store. The first thing most shopkeepers in India do is perform a *puja* inside the shop. I was interested to know with how much importance the shopkeeper treats his customers. I would typically go in when he was about to start the *puja* and see whether he attended to me first or made me wait till his *puja* got over. For a shopkeeper, the customer should be his deity and it was imperative that he was given the first priority. If they passed these two tests, I would then initiate discussions.

By the mid-Nineties our brands had become quite popular with customers and the Pantaloon Shoppe by now had been established as a complete fashion wear destination that provided value for money. It went with the tagline, 'The *surpricing* shopping experience.'

We also launched a concept called Pantaloon Cash N Carry outlets. These were warehouses set up by our distributors for small shop owners to choose our products from the shelves. That again helped increase our penetration even in local stores. There were four national distributors based in Mumbai, New Delhi, Kolkata and Chennai. For example in Kolkata, our eastern region distributor, Pradeep Saraogi had a 1,500 square feet store on Camac Street where small retailers from across the city would come and visit.

PRADEEP SARAOGI*

I first met Kishoreji through an acquaintance at Mumbai's Oberoi Hotel lobby and it was a fifteen-minute meeting. He came wearing a pair of jeans, *chappals* and a T-shirt. I didn't find him too impressive at face value but he had some kind of a magic that made me think on his terms.

---

*Pradeep Saraogi was the eastern region distributor for Pantaloon brands between 1993 and 1999 and is based in Kolkata.

Even though he asked for a huge deposit, I decided to take up his offer for the eastern region distributorship. Something I find unique about Kishoreji is that whatever he does, he does it in the biggest possible manner. When we launched the Bare brand in Kolkata, he organised a fashion show at the Oberoi Grand hotel and it was probably the biggest fashion show the city had seen that year. Similarly, when he launched John Miller, he again had a grand plan. He got models driving in motorcades across the city wearing John Miller products. During the 1996 Cricket World Cup, Pantaloon offered a car to the highest scorer. This decision worked amazingly well as Sachin Tendulkar won the car and good amount of buzz was generated around this award. This kind of advertising and marketing support is a dream for every distributor. People used to laugh at his back saying that he is being foolish in spending this kind of money. But his focus was on building the brand, whatever it took.

In a bid to establish ourselves as a fashion house, we must have got almost every leading model of the day to model for our brands or endorse them. Diya Mirza, Aishwarya Rai, Milind Soman, John Abraham and Sushmita Sen, among others, modelled for our brands much before they became famous. We spotted them early on and maybe our brands proved lucky for them!

VI

At its height there were seventy-two Pantaloon Shoppes spread across more than forty cities, including towns like Hubli, Kakinada,

Quilon, Rourkela, Trichy, Trivandrum, Udaipur, Vijaywada and Warangal. In 1994, we had a turnover of Rs 9 crore and we set an ambitious target of touching the Rs 100 crore mark within the next five years. We announced this in our annual report that year.

But even though we were increasing the number of outlets in the country, things weren't turning out the way we expected them to. By the end of March 1997, we were in for a rude shock. After increasing our topline by three times in two years, we grew by just fifteen percent in 1997. It was time for a course-correction and some deep introspection.

Large format retailing was slowly gaining ground in India. The first outlet of this kind, Shoppers' Stop, opened in Mumbai in the early Nineties. Existing legislations at that time allowed foreign retailers to enter India and a few of them were already making inroads into the market. We, on the other hand, were largely led by the franchise model. We realised that while the new franchisee outlets were driving growth, the older ones were slugging behind and in some cases actually reported a drop in sales. Clearly, there were problems cropping up with our basic model.

For one, we had made the mistake of spreading ourselves too thin. We were present across the length and breadth of the country, and that posed a logistical nightmare. Also we weren't being able to visit all our stores regularly or check what was happening there. Inventory statements and sales figures came in late. Due to lax control, we figured, we were dealing with some people who were taking unfair advantages at our cost.

The franchisees were independent shop owners and they worked on a commission basis. They owned and managed the store while we owned the stocks. Many of them focussed more on lining up their pockets rather than building a long-term relationship with the customers. There was a total lack of standardisation when it came to branding, display and customer service. For example, we decided to provide free alteration services to our customers. But often the franchisee would not inform the customer, and yet charge us for it and pocket the alteration fees. Even worse, when we launched time-bound promotions, franchisees booked past sales during the promotion period.

I suppose that many franchise operations go through this problem. To run a successful franchise model, one requires watertight agreements, strict control mechanisms and some tough rules and regulations. So we understood with some relief that our slow growth wasn't because our products were not selling, but because the model wasn't working for us.

Around this time, Rakesh, my youngest cousin, graduated from college and joined the business. He brought in a lot of fresh ideas and his youthfulness into the business. Over the years, he has also led some of the most successful initiatives that we have undertaken.

RAKESH BIYANI*

Through all the businesses, whether it was Pantaloon Shoppe, Pantaloon Cash N Carry, direct retailing or wholesale, we had our own share of learning within the organisation. All these businesses were successful, but only to a certain extent. We realised that we needed to scale up in order to survive, but none of these businesses could give us the scope that we required.

---

*Rakesh Biyani is Kishore's youngest cousin. He joined the business in 1990 and is a member of the board of Directors of Pantaloon Retail.

In the meantime, modern retail had begun to establish itself here. When Shoppers' Stop came in, we approached them and tried our best to get our brands into these stores. They were selling international brands and we thought they should sell our brands too. However, they did not wish to accommodate us and we were forced to reconsider our current and future plans.

Subsequently, we lined up three distinct possibilities. One was to transform ourselves into a mega fashion brand through huge investments in the existing setup. The second was to tie up with an international brand and market it in India in a big way. The third and most challenging was to get into retail and compete with the new chains that were coming up.

We then initiated talks with a Hong Kong based brand, Bossini. Rakesh had just got into the business and was quite enthusiastic about it. He drew up big business plans for the brand in India and then we went to Hong Kong to negotiate with Bossini. However, after prolonged negotiations, our talks failed. I had, somewhat immaturely, walked out of the negotiation room. We were pretty much back to square one.

By now we were quite desperate to give a new direction to our business. We invested heavily in technology and brought in a lot of professionals in the areas of supply chain management, systems and IT. We also launched a loyalty programme, Pantaloon Privilege Club at all our stores. But I was convinced that the organisation had to take a giant leap. Piecemeal efforts wouldn't work in such a situation.

Mission Statement

ANNUAL REPORT 1995, PANTALOON FASHIONS (INDIA) LTD.

We share the vision and belief that by improving our performance through innovative spirit and dedication, we shall serve our customers and stakeholders satisfactorily. We shall be the trendsetters in fashion and offer a fair deal to all our customers. The company shall strive to be the Indian Retailing Conglomerate, with a commitment to quality.

ANNUAL REPORT 1996, PANTALOON FASHIONS (INDIA) LTD.

Pantaloon Fashion House is reinventing itself and getting ready for the retailing revolution that is going to set in the country. Our mission to be the 'Indian Retailing Conglomerate' is now taking shape.
...

The company is also venturing into a new concept of 'Retailing' which shall be spread across more than 2,500 square feet of space. It will be called 'The Mega Store' and will house everything in clothing. Two stores of this kind, totalling around 10,000 square feet, should be operational this year.

Sometime in mid-1996, we took the decision to explore how and where we could set up large format retail stores. For want of a better name, we started referring to it as 'The Mega Store.' Whenever I would visit a city, I would look around for an ideal location for situating it. Among the cities where our brands were doing very well were Hyderabad, Kolkata, Chennai and Nagpur.

One of our oldest and best running Pantaloon Shoppe was at Hyderabad's Model Town in Punjagutta. In Kolkata and Chennai, we had invested heavily in building our brands and we were reaping good dividends.

I used to visit Kolkata very often and had checked out every market and shopping district in the city. Along with my friend, Sudhir Bhandari I must have visited hundreds of outlets. One day, on our way back to the airport, he mentioned a 10,000 square feet property coming up at Gariahat. I immediately asked for the car to be turned around to head towards the location. We reached there by 8 p.m.; the doors were closed and we found that it was being converted into a marriage hall.

I felt very strongly that this was just the kind of setting I had been looking for. It was situated on one of the broadest roads of the city and was right in the middle of a throbbing shopping district. It had a good façade and the customer didn't have to climb steps to enter the shop. A flight of stairs right at the entrance, I felt, alienates a certain set of customers from the store. Maybe they find it intimidating or elitist and get the feeling that it is 'not my kind of store.' However, the rich marble flooring and the ornate wooden doors that had been designed for a marriage hall were not suitable for the kind of store I was planning.

SUDHIR BHANDARI*

The moment Kishoreji entered the Gariahat store, he said, 'I want this.' The property was huge, measuring 10,000 square feet. At the time the largest showrooms in the city

___

*Sudhir Bhandari is an old friend and associate of Kishore. He is also the MD of Kolkata based Dolphin Publicity.

were between 1,500 and 2,000 square feet. For the next two to three months, I didn't hear from him about the property and I assumed that nothing was going to happen. But in the third month, he suddenly called up and said that he wanted to speak to the owner of the property. Now the owner, Mr Shyam Sunder Dhanuka didn't have a high opinion of Pantaloon. He also owned a large apparel store in Kolkata's New Market and in the past, we hadn't been able to convince him to stock Pantaloon products there. I persuaded Dhanukaji to go to Mumbai, see how Pantaloon was doing and check whether their plans were for real. Kishoreji had told him that The Mega Store would only sell Pantaloon brands and Dhanukaji was sure that this plan wouldn't work in such a large store. But Kishoreji was adamant and sure of his plans. He is open to suggestions, but once he decides on anything, he isn't willing to change it.

SHYAM SUNDER DHANUKA*

We had purchased the property for setting up our own store. But due to some unfortunate circumstances in the family, we had to drop the idea. We were then planning to convert it into a marriage hall or rent it out to someone. It was at that point I was introduced to Mr Biyani. At that time, Pantaloon was a small brand and wasn't that well recognised. We were quite hesitant, but still initiated the

---

*Shyam Sunder Dhanuka is the landlord of the Pantaloons outlet in Gariahat, Kolkata. He is also the owner of the Sumangal store in the city.

dialogue. I then visited Mumbai with a draft agreement and met up with Mr Biyani.

During the discussion I mentioned that we were planning to open a similar Raymond store in Kolkata's Lindsay Street and had even met Raymond's Managing Director. He immediately asked why I preferred Raymond. When I said that they enjoyed a lot of goodwill, he said, 'In five years we will cross Raymond's turnover.' I thought it was not possible but I didn't argue with him. The discussion ended there. But I think he did manage to cross Raymond's textile turnover much before those five years.

Somehow, he had an infectious sense of ambition and a very positive attitude. I had written down some stiff terms and conditions, all of which he willingly agreed to. Over the next couple of months, I waited for the store to open before giving him any feedback.

I am not sure whether Dhanukaji was at all convinced of our plans. He, however, agreed to give it to us on rent, albeit at a very high rate. It was also agreed that a certain percentage of our daily sales would go to his bank account, just to make sure we didn't default on the rent. These were tough conditions, but what I got in the bargain was a perfect spot to build my dream on. It was now in my own hands to script my success story.

The New, New Thing

ॐ

'Despite all the difficulties, all the frustrations,
there is a joy in having done something as well as
you could and better than others thought you could.'

J.R.D. TATA

I

It was the morning of 8th August 1997 and the location was Gariahat, Kolkata. We had been working over there for the last two months to convert a marriage hall into a modern shopping centre. It is hard to believe today, but shopping malls were a relatively unknown concept even till the late Nineties. The stakes for us were very high because it was the ground zero of our ambitious plans to start a retail chain. The store had to open at seven in the evening and suddenly things seemed to be falling apart.

The previous evening the sign fabricator had come over, only to assure us that he would put up the signboard by noon the following day. He used to dress like a *pucca* British gentleman, complete with suits and a hat — the kind of person I suppose you will find only in Kolkata. At noon the next day, he was nowhere to be seen. It was a fifteen feet long signboard with brass letters and neon lights behind it. Unable to trace him, we started to remove the scaffolding and put up the sign ourselves. One of our colleagues rushed to the market to hire a drill gun. While they were drilling holes on the marble slab, a loud noise attracted everyone's attention. And we saw smoke coming out from a corner of the store. The electric cables had got overloaded and the fuse had blown off. Thankfully, it was near the side entrance. So the electric supply staff was called and we also arranged for a generator set. By the time the store opened, the connection had been restored.

If this wasn't enough, something else cropped up on another front. The worker who was laying the carpets had come at three in the afternoon and by five, he put on a crisp shirt and got ready to leave. I stopped him and asked where he was going. He said the place was too hot as the air conditioning wasn't working and that he couldn't work under such conditions. Besides, it was five in the evening — the time at which all factories close in Kolkata — and so he wanted to leave. Someone called up his supervisor but he too couldn't help matters. Finally, we set up a fan for him and he grudgingly agreed to finish his work.

Those days, a store launch was a big event for us. And this was our first store. We had painted the city red with hoardings and full page newspaper ads to make it a grand occasion. More than fifty friends and relatives had come over to Kolkata and around a thousand acquaintances from the city had been invited to the launch party. Now that we open new outlets almost every week, the whole jamboree around a launch has pretty much become a thing of the past. However, what remains the same is the chaos and confusion that immediately precede a store opening. But our seasoned project management crack-team by now effortlessly ensures that deadlines are hardly missed.

SUDHIR BHANDARI*

Few weeks before the launch Kishoreji again did something that was quite unusual. The company's turnover was then Rs 47 crore but he had the gumption to say that I am going to take over Kolkata. Around a hundred hoardings were booked across the city and for three months, weekly full-page ads were released in the city's two English dailies.

---

*Sudhir Bhandari is an old friend and associate of Kishore. He is also the MD of Kolkata based Dolphin Publicity.

The scale and size of the ad campaign was unprecedented in Kolkata and everyone thought it was yet another foolhardy step.

And then he added his own flair to it. To define (who at that time was) a 'Calcuttan,' he said that a Calcuttan is really proud of his city, so why not borrow the old saying, 'What Calcutta thinks today, India thinks tomorrow.' This was a complete coup and the perfect recipe for success in that city. Even today many presume that Pantaloon is a Kolkata based company and Kishoreji is from Kolkata.

Even before the store had been inaugurated, many had dismissed it as too big to operate profitably in a city like Kolkata. A 10,000 square feet store looks awfully small today and the Kolkata store has now been extended up to 27,000 square feet. But at that time, the largest stores in the city were no bigger than 4,000 square feet and ours was more than double that size. But the response it got on the first day itself silenced most critics.

Potential customers had been noticing the hectic activity going on at the location for quite some time. The Durga Puja shopping season which was about to begin proved to be the right time to launch the store. The store was thrown open to customers at ten the next morning and it got packed with eager shoppers in no time at all.

At the end of the day, our store manager took the cash to a branch of the State Bank of India located right next to the store. We had an account there, but the bank manager flatly refused to accept the cash. He explained that he didn't have a person who would sit down and count so much money!

JACOB MATHEW*

While we were working on launching a Pantaloon Shoppe in Vijayawada, Kishoreji called to say that he had got a large space in Kolkata. He asked, 'Can we design it and open a Mega Store next month?' It seemed impossible — there were no project managers or experienced professionals who could manage the opening of such a large store in such a short time.

In fact, even the name wasn't fixed till a few weeks before the launch. I guess it was two weeks prior to the launch when one night we were holed up in one of his friends' office in Kolkata. It must have been two in the morning and there was Kishoreji, Rakeshji, one or two other company people and myself. Everyone in the office had left, but we were stuck debating over the name of what we had till then referred to as The Mega Store. Different names were being tossed around: Pantaloon Fashion House, PFH International, etc. Finally, at three in the morning Kishoreji leaned back in his chair, nearly fell off and yelled 'Pantaloooooooooons.' That is, simply Pantaloon's, but without the apostrophe!

For the next half an hour, we had some heated arguments on the merits and demerits of such a name. Finally Kishoreji said, 'I have thought it all, nothing doing, we will call it Pantaloons,' and that ended the discussion. Now that was

* Jacob Mathew is the co-founder of Bangalore based Idiom Design & Consulting. He has been associated in the design, layout and positioning strategy for most formats of Pantaloon Retail.

typical Kishore Biyani. He isn't one to get stuck at taking a decision. However big or small, good or bad, a decision, if it has to be taken, will be taken.

After the launch in Kolkata, over the next six months we launched new stores in Hyderabad, Chennai, Bhubhaneshwar and Nagpur. Pantaloons outlets had the tagline, 'Where India Shops for Value' and they were positioned as 'family stores' that offered a complete range of apparels for men, women and children. Some stores also had books, stationery, toys, gifts and household items and soon cosmetics, jewellery, sportswear and footwear were added.

Many people find it strange that we chose Kolkata to launch our first large store. In the Nineties, the city was known more for industrial disputes and *bandhs*. I have always been an optimist and my sense was that the situation was at its worst. From there on, I knew it could only get better. I was proved right, and since 1997, we have grown along with the city and immensely benefited from its steady transformation.

Amidst all the negative perception, few noticed the fact that the city's population and the size of the consumption market was comparable to Mumbai or Delhi. Moreover, the rents were low and Kolkata had a large base of educated and skilled manpower. Apart from all this, there was yet another reason why Kolkata proved to be a very good launch pad for our retail plans.

Far away from the scrutiny of investors, competition and the media, we felt Kolkata would be a good place to field-test our new model. Not only did it allow us to experiment, but also gave us the time to examine and correct our course, if required. Ever since, for most new formats we launch, we bring them to Mumbai or Delhi only after they have been perfected in another city. The first store in Mumbai came up only in August 1999.

As an organisation, we have been closely associated with Kolkata since the very beginning. I think, we were quite successful in creating a good emotional connect with the people in Kolkata. The amount of respect from the business community and the loyalty that we enjoy from shoppers in Kolkata is almost unparalleled. Few years later, when we launched Big Bazaar, the first store once again came up in Kolkata.

NOEL SOLOMON*

The customer response we get at this store never fails to surprise us. In Kolkata, once you win over a customer, he or she is loyal to you for the rest of their life. Most customers in and around this area know us by our first names and treat us like family members. In fact many of us have been invited to their son's or daughter's wedding. What could be more satisfying than working in an environment like this?

II

From the day Pantaloons opened, we have been offering mostly our own brands at our stores, unlike many other retail chains at the time. In industry parlance, brands owned by retailers are called private labels. A large portfolio of private labels helps us spot fashion trends and offer these at the store much faster than other apparel manufacturers. It helps us control the fashion cycle

---

*Noel Solomon joined as a trainee Salesman when the Pantaloons store opened in Gariahat, Kolkata. He is now its Store Manager.

better, since we are directly in touch with customers and can react faster. More importantly, private label apparel is either manufactured at our own factory or by our business partners. This helps us keep the prices lower and provide more value to our customers.

'Fashion' according to us belongs in the streets. It's not the sole preserve of the Page 3 elite or ramp models. Everyone makes a statement with what he or she wears and it is evident in their day-to-day attire, whether it's bought from a large shop or off the local bazaar. And, if fashion is for the larger public, it has to be inspired from the local context. Rather than following trends set outside our country, fashion needs to flow from within our indigenous culture, customs and colours.

KRISHNA THINGBAIJAM*

Pretty much from the very first day I joined, KB talked about 'Indianising' fashion design. He was a firm believer in reaching out to the public. To him, design was not just about products or aesthetics; but about touching the maximum number of people and making an emotional connect with them.

Conventional design thinking is based on, 'let us make something that pleases us and then we will try to fit it in through promotions and advertising.' I don't think as designers many of us appreciated a demand-led approach or recognised what customers wanted. Also, we are trained in western fashion. We knew the Versace or the Gucci style,

---

*Krishna Thingbaijam is Chief Designer at Pantaloon Retail. He joined the company in 2002.

but not 'Hindustan.' Indian body sizes, skin colour and lifestyles are significantly different from people in the west. For instance, most designers do not consider the fact that most customers travel in trains and buses and not in air-conditioned cars. So, garments for Indian customers needed to be designed keeping specific Indian conditions in mind. From the very beginning, KB kept saying, 'look at our people, understand them and talk to them in their language.' It took quite some time for this to filter in. Unlearning takes time but KB ensured that it happened. Thanks to him, I am now an ardent fan of Bollywood movies as well!

At Pantaloons, we made a conscious effort to blend the Indian context into everything we offered, be it women's western wear or men's formals. For example, one of our recent summer collections was based on the idea of 'Lemon-Mirchi,' inspired from the local bazaars. Lemon and green chillies are used in India to ward off evil. At the same time, yellow and green signify freshness. The customers loved it and it became one of the most successful seasonal collections we have launched so far.

Fashion or for that matter retailing is not just about selling products — it's about selling an idea. Why do people shop when they are depressed or bored? Not just because they have money to buy, but because they want to go through an experience. Why do you buy an ice cream? Not because of hunger, the reason goes much deeper. What is very crucial in retailing is to make customers relate to every product that we are selling as well as the store environment.

Fortunately, we picked up the concept of visual merchandising very early on. Visual merchandising is an art by which a retailer makes the store talk to its customers. The colours, signage, lights, look and feel, everything is taken into account. It is very important to figure out what is the story, the picture, the idea that we are selling to our customers. When we started to interpret our stores in this way, customers got more attracted to them and to our products.

Another concept we incorporated early on was that of 'category management,' as opposed to the brand merchandising practice that is followed by many retailers. Category management is based on the belief that a customer walks into a store looking for party shirt or a formal trouser, rather than a particular brand. Therefore, the store is designed according to categories like men's formal wear, women's western wear or casual wear, etc. Within the organisation too, teams were divided according to the categories that they managed, rather than the brands. We wanted to have a complete bouquet of products in each category at different price-points, design, fabric, size and colour. The objective was to create 'traffic drivers' within the store rather than make brands compete with each other. Focussing on categories also helped us achieve a level of perfection within the specific segments.

Today, Pantaloons targets an upwardly mobile, young, aspirational customer and goes with the tagline, 'Fast Fashion.' The middle-aged mother walks into our stores expecting value for money and her daughter comes in because she finds it fashionable. The idea has always been to ride on two winning retail propositions — being in fashion and effective pricing.

But 'being in fashion' is much tougher than it seems. The usual formula of buying everything at a low price and selling it doesn't work in this case. Fashion is highly perishable and if it isn't sold within a particular time frame, it has to be sold at a discount. It's quite like a fish market — if you don't sell your fish within the first few days, when it's still fresh, you aren't left with any option but to sell it at a discount and free up the space.

What this therefore demands is shorter 'lead times' or what we call the shorter mind-to-market. The time between recognising fashion trends and putting them on the store shelves, has to be as less as possible. It involves identifying a trend, conceptualising it, preparing samples of it and understanding its business viability. Next, orders are placed for the fabric, followed by manufacturing. Simultaneously, work on the store design and the visual merchandising has to begin and be completed by the time the products are dispatched from the factories for the stores. The challenge is to complete this entire cycle within six weeks. In order to streamline and hasten this process, we are working on an innovative team environment. And with seven seasonal collections, we are close to meeting this target.

III

Though we entered modern retail at a fairly early stage, we were not the first entrants. During the 1980s, there were a few chains already operating, like Akbarally's and Benzer in Mumbai; Spencer's in Chennai; Kid's Kemp and Nilgiri's in and around Bangalore. But these were restricted to a single city and the few national chain of stores belonged to the textile companies, Bombay Dyeing, and Raymond.

Among the first retail chains was Shoppers' Stop and by the turn of the century they had four outlets. In 1998, the Tata group company Trent, bought over a UK based chain's retail outlet Littlewoods, in Bangalore. They renamed the store Westside and opened three more stores by the end of 1999. Globus opened its first store in 1999 in Indore and followed it up with another store in Chennai in the same year.

Most of the chains set up at that time are now counted among the leading retailers in the country. These were mostly promoted by established business houses and were run by professionals. Everyone in the sector went through a steep learning curve during this period. Heavy discounting of unsold merchandise and lack of quality retail space turned out to be severe roadblocks in the expansion of most retail chains. And there were also some players who made a steady exit out of the sector.

VED PRAKASH ARYA*

Retail is a hundred piece puzzle wherein a lot of times you have to bet on the unknown. One doesn't know whether a particular merchandise or a particular store layout will work or not. It's quite unpredictable and even if a customer is visiting your store today, she may not come in tomorrow. One can't achieve a sense of perfection, because what a customer finds perfect today may seem unappealing tomorrow. As a retailer one has to reinvent oneself almost every day. To do that, a lot of decisions have to be made on the spur of the moment and closer to the shop floor. One also has to continuously grow the business and drive innovation.

---

*Ved Prakash Arya is the Chief Operating Officer and member of the board of Directors of Pantaloon Retail. Prior to joining Pantaloon Retail in March 2004, he served as CEO of Globus for six years.

However, during the first phase of modern retailing in India, most companies approached it from the traditional way of working, focussing on profitability, rather than on growth and being very cautious with their expansion plans. They formed traditional structures wherein all function heads came together and decisions were made in a bureaucratic manner. Retail however can't be managed that way. Globally, every successful retailer had an entrepreneur driving the business during its initial phase. The entrepreneur provides the big picture and decisions are taken by everyone in the organisation.

I had known KB for quite sometime during my stint as the CEO of Globus. Whenever he would visit our store, he would call me to say, 'My daughters seem to like your store. You must be doing a great job.' He believed and still does, that there is ample room for multiple players to coexist in retail. But I could also sense the passion with which he was building his own chain. He was the only one in the industry who was betting on the future, rather than the present. He was focussed on scaling up the business, rather than concentrating on driving efficiency and profit margins. To me, that seemed to be the right way to approach this business at that stage.

Foreign direct investment was allowed at that time and a few foreign retailers were already operating in the country. Most Indian retailers have steadily grown and earned the loyalty of Indian customers over the last decade. On the other hand, if one looks at the performance of foreign retailers who entered pre-1998, it is evident that most of them were hardly able to add any value either to the sector or to the economy.

For example, the RPG Group launched a joint venture with a Hong Kong based retailer, Dairy Farm International in May 1996, and started the Foodworld chain of supermarkets. They also had a beauty chain, Health & Glow that had six outlets in Chennai. However, in 2005, the partners parted ways and RPG Group now operates on its own.

One of the first foreign retailers during those days was Nanz Supermarkets. This particular case is more interesting because it had not one but two foreign retailers as equity partners. Marsh Supermarkets of United States and Nanz AG of Germany along with Indian partners, the Escorts Group, set up their supermarket chain in 1993. Each partner had an equal stake in it. By 2000, there were around sixteen stores, some company owned and some franchisee outlets, mostly in and around Delhi. During this period, the company also had six CEOs — probably an indication of the difficulties the chain faced. It had to finally shut shop the same year. In 2002, an attempt was made to revive it with a new foreign investor but that too failed fairly soon.

What is evident from this period is that foreign retailers, even with their deep pockets and years of experience couldn't make much headway in India. The world over, retail is a very local business and it is difficult for a foreign player to cater to the customer base of a different country. Only a handful of international retailers have been successful across multiple countries. Retail requires a deep understanding of local tastes and preferences. As an indigenous retailer we had a strong advantage over foreign retailers within India. Within two years of launching, we had established a fairly pan-Indian presence with Pantaloons. By the end of 1999, there were thirteen Pantaloons outlets including four in Hyderabad, two in Chennai and one each in Kolkata, Vijayawada, Nagpur, Bhubhaneshwar, Thane and Pune.

IV

On the day we opened the first Pantaloons store in Kolkata our share price was Rs 6.20. Let us assume that someone had invested Rs 1,000 in buying our stock on that day and had held on to those shares. Exactly nine years later in 2006, the Rs 1,000 investment would have been worth Rs 2,62,000. Investors have now given a thumbs-up to our company's capabilities and plans, but in 1997, there wasn't a single investor who believed that this was possible.

Even though modern retail was gaining ground in the late Nineties, the concept was somewhat alien to Indian investors. We wanted to raise capital, but few in the stock markets were willing to bet on this sector. During the first few years, our job was more of 'educating' investors on modern retail and how it had grown worldwide. Till recently, we were among the only two retailers listed on the Indian stock exchange. I have no qualms in admitting that we were first 'discovered' by foreign investors and the Indian investors took notice much later. Foreign investors who had invested in retail in their home countries could clearly recognise the potential of retail in a country like India.

Among the first Indian institutional investors, who invested in our stock, was the private equity fund, ICICI Ventures. They were willing to spend time with us and understand our business before deciding to invest in it. While they do not hold any stock of Pantaloon Retail any more, we continue to have a very strong relationship with them.

NITIN DESHMUKH*

When I first met Kishore Biyani in late 1999, he was not counted among the poster boys of the sector. In fact he was considered a textile trader who had turned into a readymade garments seller and was now trying to create a mid-market menswear brand — essentially an 'also ran.' When we discussed Pantaloon as a private equity investment proposition within our team, there were a lot of concerns. Most industry references were often sceptical and not-so-charitable. Further, retail was certainly not the happening sector in 1999, nor was there any historical data or demand estimate of the potential opportunity. We still went ahead and took the risk on two counts.

One was, I strongly believed in the opportunity based on what we had seen happening across the US and Europe. I felt that it was just a matter of time before a similar boom happened in India. The timing could have been anybody's guess but with the disposable income of the average shopper increasing steadily, there was a smell in the air. People had to spend their money somewhere and modern retailing had to come in to cater to their needs. We followed this hypothesis with a passion, funding not just Pantaloon Retail but a lot of other retailers as well.

*Nitin Deshmukh was the Chief Investment Officer of ICICI Ventures between 1997 and 2001 and also served on the board of Directors of Pantaloon Retail. He is now Head-Private Equity, Kotak Mahindra Bank.

We being financial investors had the opportunity to have a ringside view of all the retail players in the country. It was evident to us that Kishore had a very good pulse of the Indian middle class consumer's spending potential. To me, Kishore seemed to be distinctly different from the rest. I found a different kind of a spark in this man that got me interested. It took a lot of time to even get him talking, but when he did, I found that he spoke with a lot of integrity, confidence and passion. I found his ideas on fashion retailing, readymade garments for women, hypermarkets, etc., quite interesting and certainly different from some of the more established names then. I liked his straight talk and gelled with him quite well, in spite of everything that we had heard about him.

But as a team we still had to overcome the negatives associated with the company and the unfavourable accounting and financial due diligence findings. When we sat across the table, there were intense debates and we listed down covenants on various issues. Kishore was restless but there was also a willingness to change. I must admit that there was a time when I was betting a lot on Kishore as an entrepreneur, rather than just as a part of the retail opportunity.

When we started to set up new Pantaloons stores in different cities and spread much faster than our competitors, many thought it was a bubble waiting to burst someday. There were others who thought that either our numbers were fudged or we were plain lucky. Within a year or two, many predicted, we will have to shut shop. I suppose every fast-growing company goes through such a phase in the beginning. It is basic human nature that when someone home-grown is on to something, his own people are the last to recognise him.

Prospective investors often had a long list of complaints. These had either to do with the fact that we were selling mostly private labels, or that the expansion plans were extremely risky, or that we had negative cash flows. We were in a tearing hurry to expand, and these characteristic textbook responses, used to analyse steady-state companies, could not deter us. Rolling out retail stores guzzled up cash much faster than it could generate — at least, not immediately — and to make matters worse, we took debts up to our eyeballs.

Private equity investors at that stage took a broad call on the sector and invested across multiple retailers, including us. But we were also fortunate to have a group of long-term individual investors who started believing in us. All of them had visited our stores and were prepared to focus more on the number of customers coming in, rather than the financial numbers on the balance sheet. Instead of taking a 'spray and prey' approach, they invested only in our company.

One of the first was a Bengali gentleman from Kolkata who happened to visit the Pantaloons outlet in Gariahat. He saw the crowds and the merchandise we were offering and started to put in his stakes. He did not get good returns in the beginning, but his trust in us was so strong that he kept acquiring our stock as well as recommending it to his friends in the investment community. In fact, most of our large investors came that way — after hearing our story from one of our existing investors.

RAKESH JHUNJHUNWALA*

The market's anxiety emerged from a lack of appreciation of retailing as a business and of Kishore as a person. He was considered over-ambitious, but they all missed the big picture as well as the bus.

Kishore was aggressive in a field that was supposed to see a lot of growth in India. The stock market was concerned about the high debt-equity ratio. But I found that it wasn't the debt that was high, it was just the equity base which was low. So we helped him raise funds through private placements.

I backed Kishore because he was very different from most entrepreneurs. First of all, he was very aggressive and secondly, he wasn't money-minded. For him achievement meant doing what he thought innovative. He understood customers well and there was a lot of clarity in his thinking. Also, he went beyond the numbers. I found this quality to be a key differentiator.

He didn't drive himself by what revenues he was going to earn but by what percentage of the consumer's wallet he was going to attract. Instead of thinking of the profits he could make, he used to wonder about the number of footfalls he could aspire for. He was someone who always had his eyes on the big picture and willing to play the game for the long-term.

By early 2000, we had actively begun work on Big Bazaar. Though it was supposed to generate higher return on capital

---

*Rakesh Jhunjhunwala is an individual investor in Pantaloon Retail.

employed, it needed still more cash to expand. At such a stage it gets very tempting to board a jet and jump across from one investor conference to another, marketing one's idea and raising money. But I don't think any number of public relations experts or natty presentations at Hong Kong, Singapore or Goa mean anything to the value of stock in the long run.

Instead, we kept Dalal Street informed about every development and brought out monthly revenue reports. We were also open about the fact that we would not pamper the demands of day traders or provide immediate returns to shareholders. Our plan was to build an indigenous retailing model. If we were successful, our investors would naturally be the biggest beneficiaries in the long run.

BALA DESHPANDE*

In any success story there will be a point where the belief in the future outweighs the risk that you are taking. However, during this phase CEOs need to be far more articulate or rather far more willing to take the pains to explain it to the markets. Kishorebhai on the other hand is a man of few words. He doesn't make slick presentations or offer glossy brochures. And since the concept itself was new at the time, it was difficult for him to convey his conviction and vision in a manner that the capital market could appreciate.

Around the time Big Bazaar was launched, the debt-equity ratio of the company shot up to 1.8 times and investors

---

*Bala Deshpande is the Director-Investments at ICICI Ventures. She is also a member of the board of Directors of Pantaloon Retail.

found that scary. But in retrospect one can say that considering the potential that Big Bazaar had, he actually didn't take much of a risk. Knowing what he was sitting on and how it has unfolded since then, it probably wasn't a risk at all. With Big Bazaar he was able to take the company on to a new orbit. It was an opportunity that was waiting to be tapped and he did it.

I think what added to the challenges that the company was facing at that point was that it happened to be a listed company and it was an open book. The analysis was far more rigorous, detailed and harsh. Technically, growth companies shouldn't be listed at that stage but the circumstances were such that the primary markets were the best way to raise money in India in those days.

What most people missed out was that the company has never defaulted on a single loan till date. Every banker was willing to lend him and that speaks a lot about the business. It needs to be traced back to the person and his credibility. For Kishorebhai, growth was important. If he had waited for the cash flow to become substantial enough to fund the growth, he would have lost the lead, if not the market. In retrospect, I believe that it was also the honesty with which he conducted himself that helped him win the trust of investors in the long run. While he shared his big plans for the future, he was also very open about his constraints and the risks that were involved.

In our experience, once an investor gets to know our company and our values, he or she doesn't hesitate to buy our shares. The people who have got the best out of Pantaloon stock are those who have studied our company, recognised our strengths, believed in our philosophy and then decided to invest for a sustained period. But it takes good amount of time and effort to build such relationships.

So, whenever someone showed an interest in our company, we would first take him or her to our stores. One of our managers would accompany them and I often joined them later in the day, if they happened to be in Mumbai. In fact, we have taken a lot of foreign investors to different parts of the city including the slums and *chawls*, and not just the shopping malls. It turned out to be a really good idea to expose them to the real market conditions. Once the armchair analysts were taken out of the confines of cosy south Mumbai hotels, they seemed to appreciate the entire scenario much better.

Since the time we got listed, we faced a lot of scepticism and discouragement. It was natural to get frustrated. At one point I seriously contemplated the option of de-listing our company from the stock exchanges. But as I look back, I realise that the journey would have been half as fun, half as stimulating, if we hadn't faced so many roadblocks. Every time we overcame a challenge, it gave us more confidence and every time we disproved a cynic, it gave us a sense of joy. Most analysts, who have tracked our company for a fairly long time, have stayed consistent in their support. Though every report still has its fair share of 'concerns' and 'risk areas,' by and large they have stood by us.

First Global Financial Services Analyst Report
October 2005

On any given day, at any given time, in Big Bazaar stores, one might find oneself jostling for space between stacks of merchandise and a sea of humanity. But post-jostling and after inching one's way down the serpentine queue at the billing counter, there's a sense of fulfilment which only comes from some fantastic, unanticipated bargain buying. We know a lot of people who love Big Bazaar ... a whole lot of them ... Pantaloon is clearly doing things right.

From a little-known name less than a decade ago, Pantaloon has grown to become one of the top players in the Indian retail industry, thanks to its savvy management with extraordinarily quick execution capability, the sheer strength of its business model and most important of all, perfect timing.

But will the wagon wheel continue to roll? Yes, there are the conventional risk areas.

Like any other company, we too wanted to keep our stock prices up and attract more new investors. We tried to balance both the short-term and long-term, and create a situation wherein the investors could first earn from their investment. When on an average, we were opening roughly 200 square feet of retail space per hour, a lot of planning had to necessarily be short-term. But to sustain that kind of growth, we had to constantly balance it with the long-term. So we based our plans on three-yearly cycles and we have so far been able to deliver on every target we set.

My belief that once someone earns from us, he will invest in our company whenever required, has proved true. Over the years we have raised substantial sums of money through rights issue and preferential allotments, and these have funded most of our expansion plans. Whenever an investor has made any suggestions we have taken them seriously. At the same time, I think we have been able to make investors understand our point of view and have tried to understand theirs.

A lot of hard work went into making people believe in our dreams and abilities. And we have been lucky to have friends like Professor Shivanand Mankekar and his son, Professor Kedar Mankekar who have seen us from very close quarters. They have not just been investors in our company, but also a sounding board for many of our decisions on finance.

SHIVANAND MANKEKAR*

Our journey with Pantaloon began in May 2002. At Bangalore's Taj Residency we were meeting a friend from the financial community at the business lounge. We were talking mostly about some of the BPOs I had visited, when he casually mentioned to us that there is something called a Big Bazaar that had opened up in the city which was worth checking out.

Later in the evening we set out to take a look at this new concept called Big Bazaar. When we entered the ground floor, it took barely three minutes for us to decide that this is the retailing model we had to own. The reason was simply the environment which greeted us — an environment of chaos where people were literally freaking out. In our quest for the right retail company to invest

---

*Shivanand Mankekar is a visiting Professor of Finance at Mumbai's Jamnalal Bajaj Institute of Management Studies. He is also an individual investor in the company.

in, we had visited several stores, but they all were focussed only on lifestyle retailing. India needed a value retailing model to revolutionise the Indian retail scene. Big Bazaar fitted the bill since here we found a customer who had driven in on a Mercedes, shop as excitedly as folks who had come on foot and the store was packed on a weekday evening! Later our local friends told us stories about downing of shutters on weekends at Big Bazaar to avoid overcrowding.

Just to confirm that what we saw wasn't sheer coincidence, we made two more visits to the store and each time it was the same situation with respect to the crowds.

After our third visit, we rushed back to our hotel room, called our broker, and asked him to buy four percent of the equity capital of Pantaloon over the next few days. We didn't do any of the typical things expected from finance professors, i.e. analyse the balance sheet or meet the management. The simple reason for this was that the Big Bazaar outlet spoke much more, it screamed out that here was a guy who really understood retailing the Indian way.

On returning back to Bombay, when we met KB, in our first meeting itself we told him that we had at least a thirteen-year investment horizon on Pantaloon, by which time we believed that Pantaloon would have a Rs 1 lakh crore market-capitalisation. KB laughed it off since on that day Pantaloon's market-cap was barely Rs 50 crore! But today, four years hence, Kishore says anything is possible. We always tell him that we believed more in him than he did in himself.

A little over a year later, on the first anniversary celebrations of Big Bazaar at Lower Parel, KB called up to say that we must come down to Big Bazaar to see the crowds that had gathered. We immediately rushed to the store and it was raining heavily. But we were amazed to see people standing outside, waiting in long queues to get in. We walked around the queues and spotted a very well dressed man, standing with his wife, holding an umbrella in one hand and a small sleeping kid in the other. We couldn't resist asking him 'Why are you waiting in the queue?' His reply was, 'Big Bazaar always gives good deals. Today is the anniversary sale, so deals will be even better. We can't miss it.' That made our eyes moist. Big Bazaar had struck an emotional chord with its customers and that day we felt a deep sense of satisfaction that the only retailing company we had ever invested in, was so deeply impacting the lives of people. The loyalty was now spreading to the customers too!

Big Bazaar proved to be an inflection point for us. With Big Bazaar we earned the admiration of the capital markets. But to me what was most important was that we were able to reach out to an even greater number of customers than ever before. It is now time to share the story of Big Bazaar with you.

For God, Country & Big Bazaar

'If at first the idea is not absurd, then there is no hope for it.'

ALBERT EINSTEIN

I

Nearly four hundred kilometres southeast of Mumbai, in western Maharashtra, is the quaint little township of Sangli. Surrounded by sugarcane fields, the town is a trading centre for turmeric, oil seeds, sugarcane and grapes. The town derives its name from s*aha galli* or 'six lanes' in Marathi. Most of its residents are farmers who own large tracts of land in the surrounding villages.

Mohan Jadhav is one such sugarcane farmer who lives in Walwa, another forty kilometres from Sangli. Fifty-five years old Jadhav lives in a joint family that has 127 members. He also happens to be our biggest customer till date. On a sunny Tuesday morning in March 2006, he drove down to Sangli in his Bajaj Trax pickup van along with his wife, sister-in-law and nephews. The six of them visited our Big Bazaar outlet in the town and indulged in some frenzied shopping activity — buying grocery, utensils, shirts, *dhotis*, saris, shoes, toys and much more. At the cash counter, his bill turned out to be fourteen feet long. The total amount he had shopped for, on a single day at this Big Bazaar outlet, was Rs 1,37,367.

Our store in Sangli is a bit different from what you would see at say, High Street Phoenix in Mumbai. For instance, it isn't air-conditioned; instead, there are air-coolers installed inside the store. Also, there are as many shoppers there on weekdays as on weekends. Unlike office-going people in big cities, people in smaller towns do not restrict their shopping to weekends. The store factors in the local tastes, preferences and culture, and in that way no two Big Bazaar outlets look the same. One will find nine-yard saris, *dhotis*, local produce, and some agricultural implements available only at our Sangli outlet. It's the only outlet where we sell even edible oil loose, because customers want it that way. Our biggest media vehicle in Sangli is the local All India Radio station. We also make announcements on auto-rickshaws that tour the town, and advertise in the four local Marathi newspapers.

Yet in a town like Sangli, there is a three-screen multiplex that screens Marathi, Kannada, Hindi movies as well as Hollywood flicks dubbed in the local language. People are accustomed to buying at self-service stores, thanks to the cooperative stores that have mushroomed in the area. Outside the stores, one will find Mercedes, Toyotas and Chevys parked next to pickup vans and mopeds. And there are lot of people like Jadhav who live in Sangli and aspire for a similar choice of brands and products that are available at High Street Phoenix. Moreover, their disposable income compares very favourably with many customers living in Mumbai.

This is not just true for Sangli; our experience has been the same in a small industrial town like Durgapur in West Bengal or a cantonment town like Ambala, in Haryana. We have found that apart from the seven large cities in the country, there are around hundred such small towns and cities that have a sizeable population of people who have a high disposable income and an aspirational mindset. The 3-C theory of change and confidence that is leading to a rise in consumption, is evident across every part of the country. All that is required is understanding and catering to their local as well as their unarticulated needs and requirements.

ANANTH RAMAN*

Whenever I am in India, I get the feeling that the vast majority of customers, even those among the well-to-do

---

*Ananth Raman is a UPS Foundation Professor of Business Logistics at the Harvard Business School. He has co-authored a case study on Big Bazaar.

families living in large cities, have not been to modern retail chains and have a perception that these places are expensive. They tend to avoid such places. And it is not completely out of place. I remember talking to the head of operations of a Peruvian supermarket chain and he admitted that when he has to buy apples, he prefers going to the local fruit market, rather than to modern stores. He appreciates the act of picking the apples, bargaining for them and he is satisfied only when he feels he has got a good deal. The *psychology* of the price and the product is very different from the price itself. In fact, a friend of mine in Philadelphia was explaining that his parents, who emigrated from Italy, still prefer to go to the farmer's market, knowing fully well that the prices are the same at the supermarkets in the city.

As academicians we like to interpret and describe shopping in terms of evolving from one steady state to another steady state. But it is the transitionary phase that is far more challenging and interesting. Indian customers are in that phase, moving from the bazaars on to modern retail. During this stage, retailers have to play the role of missionaries, and customers need a certain amount of handholding. If they don't do it, they will attract only a very small portion of the Indian customer base. To attract a mass base, retailers need different solutions and Big Bazaar is probably the best example of this solution.

For outsiders, the word 'Big' in Big Bazaar may be the more important one, but for KB, it is the word 'Bazaar' which is more significant. I think what he correctly realised is that the classical supermarket which is so typical in the west may not be something that most Indian consumers are entirely comfortable with. He follows the Indian consumer with passion and retail is all about appealing to the heart.

If one looks at Indian bazaars, *mandis*, *melas*, they are environments created by traders to give shoppers a sense of moment, of event, of place. Instead of being fancy or pretty, these places give the feel of being authentically 'no-frills.' They provide an inclusive environment where men and women from all castes, creeds and classes can come and shop at the same place.

When we started working on the idea of Big Bazaar, we were quite clear that we had to reflect the look and feel of Indian bazaars at our modern outlets, so that no customer felt intimidated in her surroundings. The perception of the common Indian till recently was: modern shopping outlets are expensive places. The swanky malls with their glitzy floors and huge glow-signs — characteristic of modern retail — are good enough to give a shopper the feeling that the products inside are overpriced. Not surprisingly, many retailers complain that most of the people who walk into a mall often don't enter any store, leave alone buy anything. Of course if you have a burly guard standing right in front of the entrance and the most expensive products showcased in the shop window, it will put off customers. If the feeling the store gives is an exclusive one, customers will be only too happy to believe that it doesn't give value for money and move on.

One may find this strange today, but when the first shopping mall of Mumbai, Crossroads opened, it only allowed visitors who had a credit card or a mobile phone. Such were the early days of modern retail in India!

HANS UDESHI*

The idea from the very beginning was to make Big Bazaar very comfortable for the Indian customer. That was Kishoreji's strength as a retailer and he was clear about two things. One, to never hire a foreign consultant because they do not know India and two, always keep the Indian customer in mind and don't force your likes and dislikes on her.

In many ways, Big Bazaar was an extension of his personality. He would say that I do not know how to wear a tie so let the world laugh at me but I will not pretend to be somebody I am not. He had a lot of confidence in what he was doing, even though it often defied conventional logic. I think the company also took on that personality. The message he was trying to put across was that the customer is queen; and if the store was lavishly done up, she would think that the store was wasting money on frivolous things rather than concentrating on giving the best value to her. It was a simple idea, but its power was immense. For example, when we were designing the uniform for the staff, a lot of people said they should look smart and wear ties, white shirts, etc. Kishoreji was completely against it and said that the salesman should never look smarter than his customer. If the customer is Grade 5 on the social ladder, let the salesman look Grade 4.

---

*Hans Udeshi was part of the initial team of Big Bazaar and served as the Chief-Category Management of Big Bazaar. He quit the company in 2006 and is now spearheading Landmark group's foray into hypermarkets.

The customer shouldn't get intimidated by the salesman, but be comfortable while interacting with him. That was amazing. It was a clear and precise idea and it said a lot. I don't think Kishoreji has himself ever worn a tie to work.

People often complain that Big Bazaar outlets always look very crowded. But few realise that it is consciously designed to look just like that. When a shop looks neat and empty, the masses never walk into it. There has to be what is called the 'butt and brush effect,' and an 'organised chaos.' As Indians, we like bumping into people, chat, gossip and eat, all while we shop. Shopping is a form of entertainment for us.

The success of Big Bazaar is not in the big sales figures it achieves or the number of stores that have been opened. To me, the fact that Big Bazaar has emerged as a classless destination where every part of the society comes together is the hallmark of its success. And the inspiration for this wasn't any foreign retail format, but a store located in Chennai's Theyagaraya Nagar.

II

During the first few years of Pantaloons, we were always pleasantly surprised by the customer response we got during the Sale season. Every time prices were dropped, customers would turn up in large numbers. The volume of sales would go up significantly enough to make up for the dip in margins. That made us think what would happen if we had a format that allowed us to have a Sale 365 days a year? At the same time, we were also looking at how we could capture a larger share of the customer's wallet. In a nascent but fast-growing sector like modern retail, we didn't want to measure ourselves only in terms of market share or benchmark ourselves against the competition. Consumption was rising at a fast pace and we focussed on attracting the maximum share of customers' expenditure towards our stores.

At Pantaloons, we were selling mostly apparel and were able to capture an eight percent share of the total annual consumption of the average customer. We started exploring how we could increase this drastically and reach the fifty percent mark. Also, we wanted to reach out to a larger customer base. Whenever I visited a city, I would spend time visiting large markets and shops to figure out how we could take modern retailing to the next level. I finally got the answer one evening in September 2000, standing outside a shop on Ranganthan Street in Chennai.

Saravana Stores is a twenty-five year old, family-run store located in the heart of Chennai and has a very simple philosophy to run its business — low margin, high turnover. Covering five floors and a basement, it stocks everything from appliances and groceries, to clothes, jewellery, toys and eyeglasses. Its textile and garment section too has everything from Kanchipuram silks to bed sheets and there is a vessel section that has loads of steel utensils. There is a separate block for fast food, where delicacies include *idlis, pooris, parottas*, soft drinks and ice creams. These are as popular as the special *laddus* and the Mysore *pauk* on offer. Located somewhat close to the railway terminus, one can see hordes of people getting in and coming out with shopping bags at any time of the day and any time of the year. It has around a hundred and twenty people just to manage the crowds but one doesn't get the best customer experience in the store. To many, Saravana may be a shopper's nightmare, but there are a lot of customers who just love it and approve of it with their frequent footfalls. I would estimate that this single shop must be doing more than Rs 200 crore worth business each year.

After studying Saravana for a couple of days, I came back to Mumbai, happy and content that we had finally found something similar to what I had in mind. What was encouraging was that such a model works and it set the template for Big Bazaar. I now focussed on building a small team that could begin the work on it and also booked space in an upcoming building in Hyderabad where I expected the first Big Bazaar to come up.

For the next few months, first alone and then with a small team, we dissected every aspect of Saravana to develop our own hypermarket model. Saravana disproved many of the accepted norms of modern retail. Unlike the hypermarkets seen abroad, Saravana showed that a store could operate on multiple floors. Also it proved my belief that hypermarkets in India have to be situated within the city, rather than in the suburbs as it is abroad. It also has to be near a transportation hub because most Indians don't own cars. Next, bags should be sealed at checkout so that people can enter and exit multiple times. Saravana also confirmed, much against the belief of many sceptics that utensils, jewellery and fashionable garments could be sold under the same roof. At Saravana it became apparent that Indians love to shop with their entire families so the stores must cater to children and senior citizens as much as young couples. And of course, that Indians come dressed up for shopping as if it's a social occasion for them!

RAJAN MALHOTRA*

I joined Pantaloon Retail as an export manager, but was soon asked to work on a new project. I remember KB

---

*Rajan Malhotra is Head, Big Bazaar. He joined the company in 2000.

saying, 'From today onwards, you won't have any designation and will be reporting only to me. We will work on a new format that will be called Big Bazaar.'

The initial Big Bazaar team comprised of the five people: KB, Hans Udeshi, who had also recently joined the supply chain function, Vishnu Prasad who was the head of south India operations, Jacob Mathew from Idiom, and me. Every week, we would travel to Hyderabad, then go to Chennai and return to Hyderabad. In Chennai, we would share rooms with KB in a guesthouse. There would be a meeting over breakfast in the morning and then everybody would go to Saravana and the nearby stores and spend time there.

Saravana gave the kick, the passion and the understanding of what Indian retail is. We saw people shopping like mad, people being herded like sheep, and then we saw them exiting with huge shopping bags. This was the real public of India and it proved the capability and capacity of the Indian consumer.

We studied everything at Saravana. We would carry a pencil and a notebook and roam inside the store. We studied their product mix, their price points, their margins and the initial merchandise matrix for Big Bazaar was a replica of that at Saravana. However, there were a few things we decided to do differently. We wanted to build a model that we could scale up and replicate fast. The margin structure and the organisational setup at Saravana didn't allow it to open new stores nationally. It was essentially a family-driven business and was being run much in the same way a neighbourhood shop is. We also wanted customers to have a better shopping experience at Big Bazaar.

People may say that we are inspired by the Wal-Marts of the world, but it was at Saravana that Big Bazaar was born. Everyone who joined the company during those days had to visit Chennai, seek homage at Saravana and then start working.

Once we had got a hold on the basic ideas that would make Big Bazaar, work started almost on a war footing. In the meantime, we also booked another large space in Kolkata located on V.I.P. Road. We wanted Big Bazaar to be a truly Indian hypermarket that offered the promise of one-stop shopping at discounted prices, targeting the price-conscious majority segment of customers. At that time, I had hardly visited any hypermarkets abroad. That in many ways helped us design something exclusively Indian.

Abroad hypermarkets are typically designed on the big-box format — spread across a single floor, with high ceilings and merchandise stacked high on racks. Shopping in hypermarkets in western countries isn't considered to be an exciting activity and customers mostly shop alone. Hypermarkets have long, narrow aisles, suitable for individuals shopping alone with carts. We realised that many of these features wouldn't work in India. For Indians, shopping is entertainment; they come with their entire families and move around in groups. In such cases, aisles can be boring, as they restrict space and can't be dramatised. At Big Bazaar, we created multiple clusters or mini-bazaars within every store. It was designed as an agglomeration of bazaars with different sections selling different categories. The U-shaped sections and islands proved to be more appropriate for the Indian context than long aisles. From early on, we incorporated factors like these that we thought helpful for our customers, into our store design.

Our first Big Bazaar outlet was supposed to come up at Abids in Hyderabad in September 2001. As luck would have it, a few weeks before it was supposed to open, the developer informed us that the completion of the mall would get delayed and store opening had to be postponed. We immediately shifted our focus to Kolkata where the second store was being planned.

DINESH SHARMA*

When we came to know that the store had to be opened before Durga Puja festival, we were all shocked. I had just joined as a trainee but everyone from the Pantaloons outlet in Gariahat had been roped into this project. The store was in a complete state of disarray. The fittings and furniture weren't ready till a few days before the store opening. Goods were all stacked on the floor. It was located on the ground floor of an upcoming housing complex and there was a broad sewage drain in front of the building. It was totally uncovered and a wide bridge over it was completed just forty-eight hours before the store opened.

Kishoreji, his brothers, Rajan, Hans and other company folks were camping at the site. It was an enterprising environment and for three days, we ate and slept inside the store. From outside, no one could have guessed that it would open so soon. But ten days before Durga Puja

*Dinesh Sharma is the Store Manager of Big Bazaar, V.I.P. Road, Kolkata.

started, we threw open the store and got a phenomenal response from customers. On the first day, some of the cash counters gave up and on the second day the entrance gate had to be repaired. Looking back, I think we could have made a lot of money betting on store openings.

Within days of the store opening in Kolkata, a foreign institutional investor paid a visit and he was reasonably impressed with what he saw. Big Bazaar brought in a lot of attention and recognition of the hard work we had put in. The first three Big Bazaar stores were launched within twenty-two days. It was also a showpiece of our speed and imagination at work.

III

The first three Big Bazaar outlets opened at V.I.P. Road in Kolkata, Abids in Hyderabad and Koramangala in Bangalore. Each location was very different from the other. V.I.P. Road connects the city with the airport and it is the classical hypermarket location — at a distance from the city centre. Abids in Hyderabad is located close to the railway terminus and the city centre and is in the old part of the city. Koramangala then used to be an upcoming locality in Bangalore. It has now completely transformed into a shopping Mecca with glitzy malls and shopping complexes.

The choice of the locations for Big Bazaar in many ways captures the essence of what we were doing — learning through experiments. What we were attempting with Big Bazaar had never been tried in India before. None of us knew what was going to work, what was right or what was wrong. We too could have waited a few years more, like many of our competitors at that time, debated, discussed, pored over data and appointed a few consultants and expatriates. Instead, we plunged into it with some amount of conviction and the intention that we will learn as we go ahead. And it did pay off quite handsomely, though not without a few hiccups.

One of our first mistakes was around the humble white shirt. Plain observation and intuition suggested that almost everybody has a white shirt in his wardrobe. Therefore it should naturally be one of the highest selling items. So we ordered around one lakh white shirts and offered these at Rs 149. The idea was to buy it low, stack it high and sell it cheap — the basic rule at any hypermarket. Customers, however, were not as keen as we expected them to be and it took us a long while to get rid of all that bulk.

Rajan Malhotra*

The mantra during those days was very simple: if you want to do something, just go ahead and do it. The power of risk-taking was given to us by KB himself. When the entrepreneur himself tells you to take the risk and do it your way, you feel inspired and compelled to act. In fact, he had warned us not to get into a situation where there was a demand, and the supply fell short.

The white shirt seemed to be a great idea and we ordered it in huge numbers. But we realised that this item, which we were so confident of, wasn't selling at all. The reason slowly became clear. The customer who walks into a Big Bazaar travels by trains and buses. Even when the price of a white shirt is low, the maintenance cost of these shirts

---

*Rajan Malhotra is Head, Big Bazaar. He joined the company in 2000.

is too high for him. As a result he doesn't get interested in this item. People who wear white shirts can afford them for Rs 499 or above and do not buy them at a hypermarket. So there was a complete mismatch between the product we were offering and the Big Bazaar customer.

By the time the first review came up, I was completely confused on how to explain this. I had tried everything — advertisements, promotions, discounts — and it still wasn't selling. During the review KB asked me what I had done. I explained that we had bought each shirt at the rate of Rs 105 and were now selling it for just Rs 129. I told him about all the other things we had tried and that none of them was yielding any result. He heard me out and then said, 'You are not trying hard enough.' I was completely taken aback, but then he added, 'Have you tried selling it at Rs 49? I know we will lose money. But we have made a mistake, let's accept it and move on.'

That incident taught me quite a few things — never fear making a mistake but if you have made one, get out of it fast and never put bad money after good money. The white shirt became our hero. It symbolised the spirit of the organisation. It was also the day when all of us became entrepreneurs. We had been given the liberty to destroy capital, something that is the sole prerogative of the entrepreneur. A manager always fears making a mistake and that is where he differs from an entrepreneur.

There are no books, consultant reports or B-schools that could have taught us the experience we had with the white shirts. It's a learning that only comes from the shop floor and when one risks making a mistake. Mistakes have been integral to our growth process. They helped speed up our learning and enhanced our sense of competitiveness. In our organisation it was always better to admit one's fault if things went wrong, rather than to seek permission at every step. Intelligent mistakes — those which happened early and inexpensively and contributed new insights about our customers — were always encouraged.

KUSH MEDHORA*

The reason why the group or the formats have been able to expand so fast is that everybody over here operates with speed and confidence when it comes to decision-making. And that's been possible because Kishore allowed people to think and take decisions on their own. The entrepreneurial instinct — even when one is an employee in the company — is very strong in this organisation. During my stint in this company, my strongest experience is that I, as an individual was allowed to make mistakes, learn from them and move forward. So I was able to take many more decisions, and work harder and smarter. Kishore's ability to see failure as a stepping-stone to success helped this company grow to what it is today.

Kishore has this amazing ability to make a person buy his dream and then build a sense of ownership in everyone who works with him. Initially, he spent a lot of time on a one-to-one basis, discussing and debating ideas and

---

*Kush Medhora heads the Projects team at the company. He used to work with Trent Ltd. before he joined Pantaloon Retail in 2004.

ensuring that we were on the same plane. Then he literally abdicated the whole projects function to me. It had a cascading effect and today I try to delegate as many decision-making powers as possible to the next level.

For retailing in general and more so in a diverse marketplace like India, one has got to build one store at a time. One just can't copy-paste one store design or merchandise mix across all stores. One has to understand local consumers and build customised models for each community one operates in. And that is possible only when the zonal heads or the local project manager have the power to take decisions.

As we expanded into new cities and started to serve new communities, it was clear that we couldn't apply the same set of rules to every store. Shopping is a local experience and habit. Moving from the neighbourhood shop to a large-format, self-service, modern retail outlet involves changing that basic habit that most people have grown up with. And every community behaves differently to this change. Therefore, it became imperative for us to not only understand each and every community but also make decisions at the store level based on the insights we got.

For example, even before we opened shop in Gujarat, we came across a common joke in retailing circles. Retailers said that a customer in Gujarat is prone to asking, 'Where is the fifth *anna* in the *rupaiya*?' Not surprisingly, many retailers consider Gujarat to be the 'Waterloo' of Indian retail. It is said that if a retailer is successful in Gujarat, he can succeed anywhere in the country.

What we discovered on launching our store there was that a customer in Gujarat is not only value-conscious, he or she has habits that are peculiar to the state and are hardly seen anywhere else in the country. When it comes to staples, the Gujarati customer prefers to buy the entire year's requirement at one go. Staples are stored in a loft, a common feature in most homes in Gujarat. Since she buys it in bulk, she also demands a heavy discount, expects it to be delivered at her home and wants to pay back on credit. And when she comes to buy her staples the following year, she expects the grain to have exactly the same characteristics or be from the same farm it was procured from last time. All these pose a tremendous challenge for a modern retail format to address. One has to constantly find out creative solutions to meet these demands. And when we were able to live up to these demands, we found a huge market just waiting to be tapped.

However, as one moves beyond Gujarat, one realises that every state, every community has its own set of peculiarities. Customers in Bengal look for an emotional connect and are also very loyal to existing brands. This makes it very tough for a new brand to establish itself. On the other hand customers in Punjab have a very high disposable income. It is also among the very few states in the country where by and large, conspicuous consumption is not associated with guilt. But customers are hardly loyal to any particular brand, product or store and make frequent changes in the choices they make. Both these communities therefore provide unique opportunities and pose tough challenges. To understand and benefit from the diversity of Indian consumers, we therefore set up a diversity tracking cell that tracked local customs, festivals, habits and consumption patterns. We left it to the store manager to make a lot of decisions based on local tastes and preferences, and customise our offerings depending on what the customers in a particular region wanted.

The chief reason why our hypermarket model worked was that we decided to focus more on merchandise rather than on operations. And this was a lesson straight out of Sam Walton's book, *Made in America*. The book states, 'In retail, you are either operations driven — where your main thrust is towards reducing expenses and improving efficiency — or you are merchandise driven. The ones that are truly merchandise driven can always work on improving operations. But the ones that are operations driven tend to level off and begin to deteriorate.' To me this was the biggest secret that Walton shared in his book.

IV

'*Is se sasta aur accha kahin nahi*' (Nowhere is it cheaper and better.) Nothing captures the spirit of Big Bazaar better than this one-liner. It is a simple statement and yet it positioned Big Bazaar at the top of the Indian customer's mind. It showed that Big Bazaar was built on the foundation of entrepreneurship and simplicity.

The initial Big Bazaar sourcing model was entirely dependent on consolidators. These people were dedicated traders. They did not have fancy educational qualifications or work experience with a blue-chip company, but understood the market far better than the so-called professionals. Apart from apparel there was hardly any category in which we had a superior knowledge base. So we appointed eight consolidators to take care of sourcing for categories like plastics, utensils, luggage, furnishings and furniture, general merchandise, etc. We gave them a broad matrix of the products we wanted, the targeted cost price and the margins we expected. Based on this they bought goods on our behalf and earned commissions on the supplies.

Consolidators were people who knew the intricacies of a particular category very well and had an industrial background. For example, the gentleman doing our apparel sourcing, Sandeep Poddar was a Mumbai based mill owner turned trader. His company, Adhunik Synthetics used to manufacture and market Adhunik brand shirt pieces. Similarly, someone who was in charge of plastics, utensils and luggage had a background in plastics manufacturing. At that time, since we didn't we have the knowledge at the company level we had to create a cost of learning. We needed people who knew their area of expertise threadbare and would act with speed. Consolidators were given a free hand and they helped us develop this knowledge base.

The consolidators were not just involved in procuring our goods; they also warehoused it and transported it to the Big Bazaar outlets. The entire back-end was being taken care of by traders who were willing to work till midnight or deliver goods to our store on a Sunday morning in their own vehicles, just to ensure that the demand of customers was met promptly. On the other hand, it allowed us to focus where a retailer must focus — the front-end. We concentrated all our energies on how we could serve our customers in the best possible manner.

While the big categories were handed over to consolidators, there were still some small categories that we were not very comfortable with. At that time, we hardly understood the business of opticals, pharmacy, books, tailoring and crockery. However, these had to be present within a hypermarket to provide a complete bouquet of products. For these categories, we roped in strong local retailers and gave them space within the stores. These were called shops-in-shops and operated on a commission basis.

Few months later, when we opened the first Food Bazaar within a Big Bazaar in Lower Parel, we took this strategy a step further. Staples, vegetables and fruits are important categories but also very difficult categories to manage. Retailers usually have to source them from the *mandis* and APMC (Agricultural Produce Marketing Committee) markets where only long established traders can do business. More importantly, food is an extremely localised business and a tough market to follow.

So in Mumbai, we tied up with the largest wholesaler at Vashi APMC for vegetables and one of the largest wholesalers from Crawford Market for fruits. They were given to manage the entire back-end as well as keep their own people to manage the category within our stores. It simplified our business. Food Bazaar and Big Bazaar developed and expanded without us getting involved in the intricacies of each category and the company could focus on appealing to the customer.

DAMODAR MALL*

It is important to realise that in the food business the margins may be comparatively lower but the 'per square foot' sale can be quite high. What Food Bazaar did was to keep the back-end simple and concentrate on teasing the imagination of the customer at the front-end. That ensured the high volume of sales for its business. At this stage of evolution most food retailing chains made a beginning with the idea that food business is a supply

---

*Damodar Mall is President and CEO, Food Business Division. He joined the company in February 2005.

chain game. They set up a strong back-end, warehouses, distribution centres and more processes and systems.

Food Bazaar, on the other hand, appealed to the customer in a very different manner. It focussed on connecting with the housewife or the homemaker and on front-end innovation. It touched the necessary chord with the customer. And connecting with the customer is especially important in the food business, because what you are selling is otherwise available anywhere else. Saying that I am bringing your shampoo in lesser time to my shelves or I know how much stock should be there on my shelf doesn't work. The customer doesn't care whether you got it on time or predicted the demand correctly. The retailer has to fire the imagination of the customer and make her buy. I think Food Bazaar did that brilliantly.

Food Bazaar deliberately kept the sourcing model very simple. It freed up management energy as many external businessmen shared the burden of procuring, storing and transporting the goods. It became a platform for amalgamation and KB left a lot of value to be shared with these traders. He operated on the principle that it was not about slicing the current opportunity but about growing it further. He was able to convince them that if collectively they were able to grow the opportunity a modern retail format provided, there could actually be three winners — the customer, the vendor and the company.

In the meantime the category team was being built and they started picking up the specialised knowledge. Finally, the customer was going to come because of the brand Big Bazaar and Food Bazaar. Understanding what the customer wanted and adding it to the merchandise mix would obviously yield good results. After I moved in, we started adding new features to Food Bazaar like a live kitchen, a pickles bar, etc.

If KB had his way, he would have liked a cow to be there at the store as well, but we didn't allow him to go that far. However, at some locations we even pasteurise milk within the store. Thanks to our focus on the front-end innovation, Food Bazaar is now a concept that runs independently of Big Bazaar. It is a model which can now be taken to the next level. We are looking at a gourmet and a hinterland version of Food Bazaar.

Damodar took around a year before he made up his mind to join us. He had been leading Hindustan Lever's retailing initiative, Sangam. But prior to that, he had gone through his own entrepreneurial experience. He had set up a small grocery chain, Apna Ghar in Mumbai, which he later sold to another upcoming retail chain. He brought with him a very strong understanding and empathy of Indian homemakers. There were times when we disagreed but most of the time our views completely matched on what was required for the Indian market.

The job of a retailer is to create demand. Building a robust supply chain is important but it is not the primary role of a retailer. It isn't enough for a retailer to have an adequate supply of potatoes; he also has to ensure that customers buy them. By focussing on the customer, we kept our business model simple, agile and open to adaptation. We may be criticised for lack of systems and processes, but local sourcing has helped us keep stocks on our shelves and cope with erratic and often unpredictable shifts in demand from consumers. A centralised process may not necessarily work for a vast and diverse country like India. It isn't easy to forecast demand for each product at each store sitting in the head office or even the zonal offices. Our store managers enjoy a lot of freedom when it comes to deciding the merchandise and product-mix at the stores. Our hypermarket model is based on the principle of building and strengthening the front-end, creating demand through the front-end and letting the supply follow.

ANANTH RAMAN*

In a business like retail, the primary concern should be how to understand and interpret customer needs and anticipate what they want. No doubt one needs a good supply chain, but it shouldn't be at the cost of understanding the customer. If I were the CEO of a chain like Big Bazaar, I would focus on current and emerging consumer trends. You can always tinker around with the supply chain at the next stage, but you can't blow up consumer understanding.

Retail has to have a right-brain and a left-brain component. It cannot be just the left-brain stuff. I once asked a very senior executive at a leading Japanese retail store, what he was concerned about. And he said his organisation was too disciplined. It was a sales-driven organisation, but it wasn't driving sales.

---

*Ananth Raman is a UPS Foundation Professor of Business Logistics at the Harvard Business School. He has co-authored a case study on Big Bazaar.

This misconception that supply chain is the be all and end all of modern retail tends to be an oddly Indian concept. In fact I can't think of a successful retailer in the world for whom supply chain was most important. Having said that, I really doubt whether the existing supply chain at Big Bazaar is the supply chain of the future. Big Bazaar cannot have so many authorised distributors who end up supplying to individual stores. At some point, the supply chain has to ensure that the goods are delivered to a central warehouse from where they are then distributed.

But not messing with the traditional Indian supply chain at this point is a good idea. It is far better to take time to understand customer needs and demands and then build a supply chain rather than jumping into it from the very first stage. Despite being a professor of supply chain management, I would suggest not to make supply chain the number one priority.

We are now about to open our fiftieth Big Bazaar store. Yet, every store that we open is an evolution — an evolution of our understanding of our customers, and an improvement of what we find works with customers and what doesn't. However, the front-end model for Big Bazaar and Food Bazaar is far more mature and it is therefore time for us to consolidate our back-end as well. During the initial years of operation itself, our category teams have been gaining a good understanding of market dynamics and can now function independently. We are now building strong logistics capabilities across our businesses that will be good enough to support our own requirements as well as those of many of our supply partners. We are also bringing in global expertise that will help us scale and replicate this model faster.

The challenge for us is that as we grow in size and scale, we have to ensure that our supply partners grow faster and are able to meet our demands. We are working with them, funding them and mentoring them towards this end. For example, in staples we have brought together our partners and formed a company that will supply quality products to our stores. We are investing in automation and technology for this company. We are helping the company hire senior professionals, so that it can grow fast and keep pace with our own growth and requirements. Besides, we have raised a private equity fund, Indivision, that can invest in small and medium companies and brands, and scale up their business. These companies have the option of becoming our supply partners and leverage our distribution network to scale up their own brand value.

However, Big Bazaar will continue to depend a lot on small and medium suppliers. A large portion of what we sell at our outlets caters to local tastes and these products have to be sourced locally. India has one of the best micro-entrepreneurial setups in the world and the power of micro-enterprise to cut costs and drive efficiency is unparalleled.

At Dharavi in Mumbai we found shirts being stitched, packed and transported to retailers at the retail price of Rs 99 per shirt. Interestingly, in such cases diseconomies of scale set in. If we were to add scale to it, bring it out of Dharavi and set up a big factory, the overheads would increase and prices will automatically shoot up. We found someone who makes lighters for Rs 5 and someone who makes disposable mud *tawas* with a non-stick coating at Rs 10. At hypermarkets in the US, the lowest price for pair of jeans is $9.99. In India, it can be got at the retail price of Rs 199 or even less. If one were to visit these areas, one would notice lakhs of such jeans being manufactured and sold everyday at Ulhasnagar in Mumbai and Gandhi Nagar in Delhi.

Forty percent of children's wear in India is manufactured at Metiabruz in Kolkata. Many families are fully engaged in this industry. The men and women design and stitch the garments while their children attach beads and flowers to them. The entire family derives its livelihood from such a micro-enterprise. I think the challenge for us will be to leverage these micro-entrepreneurs and create an environment wherein our customers benefit, these entrepreneurs benefit and we as a company benefit.

Contrary to what is generally perceived, India has pretty reliable as well as the most cost-efficient supply chain systems. Our public distribution system has 4,63,000 outlets and there are 1,60,000 post offices in India, making these part of the largest distribution networks in the world. It may not be like supply networks in developed countries, but they have their own set of advantages — low costs being the most significant of them. We have to explore how we can improve these keeping in mind the Indian context. In India a supply chain cannot depend on Volvo trucks. Instead, hand-carts, tempos and even bullock carts are hired, and they ensure that goods reach the most difficult and congested locations on time. Majority of goods delivery in India happens through bullock carts, cycles and bikes. People involved in this trade need employment and are willing to work hard to make sure that retailers get their deliveries on time, at every location. It is important for modern retailers to accept this ground reality and work with the advantages it provides.

Many modern retailers would like to believe that the days of the *kirana* or the neighbourhood shop are numbered. Nothing can be farther from the truth. We are a nation of shopkeepers and I believe that *kirana* shops will continue to prosper and coexist with modern retail. Traditional shops still provide a lot of advantages to the customer, that we in organised retail wouldn't be able to match anytime soon. For one, they have a personal relationship with every regular customer. In addition, they can offer credit, home delivery and customised services. They know what a regular customer wants even before she enters the store. We also can't compete directly with neighbourhood stores as their cost of operation is far, far lower than ours. Most of them do not impute their rent, salary and overhead costs.

We have found customers continuing to visit *kirana* stores irrespective of whether there is a modern retail outlet in the vicinity or not. For their monthly shopping customers go to a hypermarket, but for their daily, weekly purchases, *kirana* stores are still their first choice. Traders in India are smart people and in every location where we have opened our store, we have seen *kirana* stores improve their customer interface, their product mix and actually do more business than they did before. The market is large enough for everyone to survive and prosper. At our end, we do not believe in predatory pricing. None of our stores sell goods below the prices we have purchased them at. We haven't seen any store closed down in our neighbourhood after we have set up shop. In fact, we see a whole lot of neighbourhood store owners coming to our stores to buy products at lower rates than they get from their distributors, and then sell them to their customers.

My belief is that the threat to *kirana* stores doesn't come from external factors but from something internal. I have noticed that often the next generation of the owner of the neighbourhood store does not join the business. They possibly find it below their dignity to pursue this business. Trading, as you may be well aware, isn't a profession that is looked up to in our country.

There are more than seven million shop owners in our country and probably an equal number of small entrepreneurs who supply to these shops. With increased consumption, these numbers are only going to increase. In order to build a successful retailing model, modern retailers will need to leverage the huge power of micro-enterprise and the indigenous supply chain present in India. However, the threat today comes from multinational retailers who are infamous for using monopsony powers — aggressive buying power used by a single large company when there are a large number of small suppliers — to kill small businesses. Global sourcing, unfair trade practices and strong-arm tactics used by multinational retailers in their own countries pose a significant threat to micro-entrepreneurs in our country.

Bollywood Calling

ॐ

'I do not believe in consensus decision-making...
I do not take a vote, I make the decisions.'

RAHUL BAJAJ

I

What connects Steve and Mark Waugh, Ajay Jadeja, Sanath Jayasuriya and Hansie Cronje? Apart from the fact that they are cricketers, and that — except for Mark Waugh — all have captained their individual teams; all of them have endorsed Pantaloon brands in the Nineties. Cricket as an emotion touches almost every Indian and we quite successfully tapped into it for building our apparel brands. For a while I was the marketing agent in India for these cricketers and managed to get a few other brands to sign them on as well. Till that time, cricketers didn't command million dollar endorsement deals, and so we could get them to endorse a small brand like ours. We also made an attempt at launching a signature sportswear brand with Ajay Jadeja which didn't succeed. But the star-icons did play a role in establishing our identity with a certain set of customers.

By early 2000, we had started working on Big Bazaar and the focus had shifted on building a mass retailing brand based on a strong value-proposition. It was clear that if we had to succeed with a hypermarket model, we had to scale up fast and reach out to a mass customer base. More than a star appeal, a mass brand needs an emotional connect and a promise that it actually delivers on. The Big Bazaar tagline promised that we were here to offer good quality products at the cheapest price in town. And to gain the mindshare of customers, this proposition had to generate a certain amount of buzz.

There are only a handful of professionals in advertising agencies who understand, speak, and think in the language of the common people. Most marketing and advertising professionals are educated in convent schools in large metros, listen to western music, watch foreign movies and speak and think in English.

On the other hand, I was sure that I wanted to communicate Big Bazaar with one-liners in the *local* languages. At this point I came across Gopi Kukde, a relatively unknown advertising professional who hardly ever appeared in any of the glossy supplements and magazines which are devoted to tracking the advertisement fraternity. Yet, he had to his credit a large number of successful campaigns done in local languages. One of them was the famous Pan Pasand one-liner, '*shadi aur tumse, kabhi nahin!*' The good thing about Gopi Kukde is that he still thinks in Marathi and Hindi, not in English. So, for us, he used a popular Hindi phrase, '*chane ke bhaw kaaju*' (cashew nuts at the price of chickpeas) and extended it to a long list of similar comparisons — from '*rui er dame illish*' (hilsa fish at the price of rohu) in Bengali to '*stall ke bhaw balcony*' (balcony tickets at the price of stall seats), an obvious reference to movie theatres. These catchphrases appeared in hoardings and newspapers in every city where we launched a new Big Bazaar. Soon they became the talk of the town and firmly established the lowest-price proposition in the minds of our prospective customers. Everybody understood and connected easily with these simple one-liners.

GOPI KUKDE*

Ten seconds is enough for Kishore to latch on to an idea or completely rubbish it. He wanted to build Big Bazaar as a people's place where an average Indian family can come to get value for money. While the lowest-price

---

*Gopi Kukde is an ad industry veteran and has been part of the industry for over thirty years.

proposition was the central theme for Big Bazaar campaigns, he was willing to experiment and try out unconventional ideas as well. He recognised the potential of the one-liners the moment I suggested them. And later I found that he didn't shy away from courting controversies as well.

Apart from regular advertisements we also did a few promotions and activations. In one such case, we had printed hundred rupee notes in the exact size. It looked quite genuine except for the fact that on the reverse it was printed in bold, *'ab asli paise bachaiye'* (now save real money) along with the address of a nearby Big Bazaar. When we distributed these at Mumbai's Victoria Terminus railway station, it attracted massive attention of the crowds and people fell head over heels to collect them. I suppose people liked the novelty of the paper and it's always good to feel cash in one's hands, even if it is fake! But it also attracted the attention of the police.

The police arrested one of the salesmen who was distributing them and took him to the station. Later we came to know that according to the law, any piece of paper resembling a currency note had to be at least double the size of the original. I thought Kishore would blast me. Instead, when he came to know about it, he called up to say, 'Gopi, good show. That salesman was taken to the police station but he has now been released. I spoke to the inspector and explained the whole thing to him. We will do more of this ... don't worry.' Subsequently we did this in other cities as well.

Kishore can be a creative person's delight and also a nightmare. One can't predict Kishore, he is always a step ahead of what is about to be proposed. Often we had to finish a series of ads in a day's time. He insisted that fresh ads with new set of prices and products should be released every time we booked space in newspapers. And each city had to have different set of ads and communication messages. But it was fun working on Big Bazaar as one could easily notice the creative spark in Kishore. He was always thinking in terms of the mass customer and what could fire their imagination.

Communicating with Indian customers can be a tricky game. Multiple languages, multiple ethnicities, multiple religions, multiple communities make up our country, and one has to take into account all these before developing a communication strategy. There are hardly any media vehicles that reach out to every section of our society. There are also very few, if any, icons who are relevant to every Indian.

I believe that the only communication medium that comes very close to capturing the imagination of each Indian is popular films. And films have always fascinated me. The characters, the drama, the sound effects and the stunts, the songs, and the dance sequences, all come together in a film to make a billion people in our country escape their reality for three hours. Yet, in many ways movies reflect what is going on in the popular consciousness in the best possible manner.

As anyone else born in a middle class Indian family, I had grown up on a regular diet of cricket and movies. And like many other Indians, I too harboured the ambition of making my own movies through which I could communicate with the people of my country. As retailers of garments and fashion products, we were always constrained by the amount of money we could spend on advertisements. By early 2000, cricket stars and properties had become too expensive for us to afford. Movies, on the other hand, seemed to be an ideal vehicle to build our brand and take it to the masses.

A movie budget runs into at least a few crores. However, with in-film advertisements and film-merchandising, which were new concepts at that point of time, a brand message could be reached out to the huge audiences. Our thought was that if we could use this opportunity effectively, movies could become the most efficient communication vehicle for us. That's how we decided to get into the project and I handed over the execution of this idea to Vivek Singhania.

Vivek Singhania came from an established business family and had studied at the London Business School. But that wasn't the reason why he fitted into our organisation so well. He had a very creative bent of mind, had the temerity to suggest the most unconventional approaches, and was always willing to take large risks. He was also very passionate about movies and had an eclectic choice of favourite movies and directors. At times one could hear him discussing the nuances of film making that he had learnt from watching Frank Capra and Steven Spielberg's films. And a few minutes later he would seamlessly move the discussion to Sooraj Bajratya's creative genius in *Hum Apake Hain Kaun* or Shekhar Kapoor's *Masoom*. In fact, he had worked as a Line Producer in *Masoom*, had been the Chief Assistant to Vidhu Vinod Chopra and had worked on a number of other film projects.

Over the years, he had also played a key role in building our branding strategy, producing ad films for us and organising events and promotions for our brands. We formed a new company, PFH

Entertainment that would lead our foray into film making and Vivek Singhania was made the CEO of this company.

VIVEK SINGHANIA*

We were both mavericks and both of us had agreed that we would never play by the rules. We never went by NRS (national readership surveys) or TRP (television rating points) data to build our media plans. If I had a crazy thought, there was Kishore who had even crazier thoughts to back it up. We were among the first people to strike a deal with ESPN in the mid-Nineties. We had used the potential of cricket to the full extent, but as a small company, we never had enough money to support our branding strategies. I think that was what made my job more exciting and I really enjoyed working with the constraints. It brought out the best in me.

When we started our discussion about getting into films, Kishore gave me a couple of pointers. 'Make a film with which we can promote the Pantaloons store brand. It can be a regular love story that happens in and around the store. And the Pantaloons store has to be the place which young, trendy people visit.' The whole objective of the movie was to promote the Pantaloons store and enter the minds of customers. To say simply, the film was an unpaid advertisement vehicle that would reach out to all the movie-going audiences across the country.

---

*Vivek Singhania was associated with the company between 1995 and 2004. He now works as an independent producer and writer.

However, pretty much everyone including investors, family members and business associates found the idea ridiculous. As with my earlier projects, it did not bother me that I got no support for another new idea of mine. I was confident about it and could not wait for a consensus to emerge.

Apart from producing the movie, I was somewhat involved in creating the music for it as well. I also developed the marketing game plan for it. But everything related to the execution and direction of the movie was left to Vivek and a team of professionals. The most enjoyable part was getting to hear all the latest gossip of Bollywood much before the others!

II

Our first movie, *Na Tum Jano Na Hum*, was released on 10th May 2002. It had Hrithik Roshan, Saif Ali Khan and Esha Deol in the lead roles. Arjun Sablok directed the movie and Rajesh Roshan composed the music.

The movie was premiered at New Excelsior theatre in Mumbai on a Thursday evening. The premiere started a little late in the evening as some of the stars including Hrithik turned up late. When I watched my own movie being played on the big screen, there was definitely an adrenalin rush. It is a unique feeling that one gets only rarely in life. The feeling that comes with the realisation of a lifelong desire. Movies are made in a make-believe world and that experience extended during the movie premiere as well. I watched the movie along with my family, friends and the film fraternity. Almost all of them left the theatre on an encouraging note.

By Friday noon, the movie was being screened at theatres across the nation. And by the evening, the verdict was out. The box office collection figures that were flowing in suggested that the movie hadn't delivered on our expectations. Over the weekend, this trend only got confirmed. Almost a lifetime's planning and a full year of hard work had gone into making this movie. In a day's time, all those dreams and hard work had come to naught.

This sudden turn of fate happens only in the film world. Few people outside the film industry realise this, but films are probably the fastest-moving consumer goods. One can put in as much effort, as much passion, as much capital, and as many people into a film production. But how the film performs is decided on a single day, probably within a couple of hours.

What makes film making even more challenging is that no one gets a chance to correct a mistake. Unlike a product, once a movie is released there is no opportunity to correct a flaw or a drawback in any which way. On the Friday morning when a movie is released, the actors, the producers and the director of the movie are as clueless about its performance as the next person on the street. On that day, the state of mind, as I soon realised, is truly, *Na Tum Jano Na Hum* (neither you know it, nor me.)

Making a movie was probably the best experience that I had ever gone through. It was about creating something that millions of people were going to enjoy. It is a unique challenge one has to live up to and I failed it in my first attempt. It turned out to be a humbling experience and taught me lessons that shaped my life from thereon. Making a movie at that juncture may have been a mistake, but I would not have been what I am, had I not gone through this experience.

Prior to working on the movie I had believed that I knew everything about my customers. The movie proved me wrong. It was proved once again that the customer and the customer alone could decide one's success or failure. I was extremely confident about my own abilities, ideas and the subsequent success of the movie. So were many of my colleagues and associates. The movie, however, taught me that all this confidence doesn't matter. Ultimately, the verdict rested with the customer and no one else.

Since I believed so much in my own abilities to interpret and cater to the audiences' tastes and expectations, I had put in a whole lot of personal effort into it. I was extremely passionate about the movie and got attached to the project. The movie taught me that the most important thing is to never get too attached to any idea, project or concept. One has to dispassionately evaluate every business decision and realise that not all initiatives are going be successful. It is important to accept failure and to distance oneself from an idea or project if it doesn't work.

Purely from a commercial viewpoint, the movie was not a complete failure. We had not put too much money into it and therefore we did not lose any. But we did not make any money either. However, the objective of the movie — to build the Pantaloons brand — did somewhat succeed. The movie was successful in presenting a more youthful and vibrant image for the Pantaloons store brand, ultimately setting the stage for the brand's repositioning from a family store to a fashion destination for young consumers.

This was also among the first few movies that had an extensive line of film merchandise. From notebooks, folders, pens to mouse pads, we launched quite a series of movie-specific merchandise at our stores. A soft toy named 'Tutu' that featured prominently in the film, became very popular and we sold thousands of those in various sizes at the Pantaloon stores. A range of men's and

I based everything on one philosophy 'Rewrite rules, Retain Values.' Chase your dreams but don't compromise on your belief system.

REWRITE RULES · RETAIN VALUES

Yesterday

2

1 Shopping malls are a fairly recent phenomenon in India. When Pantaloon Retail opened its first store, there were hardly any shopping malls in the country. The first Pantaloons store opened in Gariahat, Kolkata in August 1997. It was housed in a building that was about to be converted into a marraige hall.

2 The first Big Bazaar in Mumbai came up at High Street Phoenix in 2002. There used to be a textile mill at this location.

Umeedon se bhari zoli

"Big Bazaar is not just the pride of our town but also a nice way to spend an evening."

Today

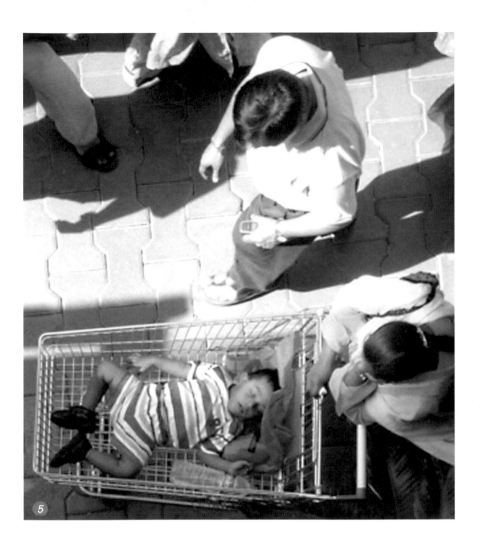

5

3 & 5 Retailing is about providing an experience, building aspirations and helping people live up to their dreams. Shopping, as one gets to learn in India, is not just about buying. Customers want to eat, celebrate, live through an experience, aspire for a lifestyle, spend time with friends and family and do much, much more within a shopping centre. And customers never cease to surprise us.

4 One of the first ad campaigns of Big Bazaar.

6a

7

Today

7 & 8 *On the* Sabse Sasta Din *there were as many customers inside the store as there were outside the store, waiting to get in.*

6a & 6b Hypermarkets abroad are characterised by long aisles. Big Bazaar on the other hand is an agglomeration of clusters featuring different product categories. It combines the look, feel and touch of Indian bazaars with the convenience, choice and hygiene that modern retail provides.

Tomorrow

rewrite rules *retain values*

FUTURE GROUP
VERTICALS
Future Retail
Future Capital
Future Space
Future Brands
Future Media
Future Logistics

CORE VALUES
Indian-ness
Leadership
Respect & Humility
Introspection
Openness
Valuing & Nurturing Relationships
Simplicity & Positivity
Adaptability
Flow

National
Retail Federation

Pantaloon Retail was awarded the International Retailer of the Year 2007 by the US based National Retail Federation, the world's largest retail trade association. While receiving the award in New York, Kishore Biyani said, 'It is a moment of pride not just for our company, but for our whole country, India. It would have been more appropriate if we had got the award after global retailers had stepped into India. We are in a no-competition scenario currently but we excel in what we do to delight our Indian consumers.'

women's apparel had also been launched under the tag 'From the sets of NTJNH.'

By the time *Na Tum Jano Na Hum* was being launched, we had already started working on a second movie, *Chura Liya Hai Tumne*. It was more of a romantic thriller set in Bangkok and had a smaller budget than the first movie. Lot of fresh talent was brought into the movie. Esha Deol who had launched her career with our first movie was the lead actress in this movie as well. Zayed Khan made his debut with this movie, as did Rakhi Sawant. Both of them featured in a song '*Mohobbat Hai Mirchi*' shaking a leg in a flashy club. The music, composed by the then relatively unknown Himesh Reshammiya, became more popular than the movie itself. Both Himesh Reshammiya and Rakhi Sawant now evoke very strong responses from everyone. People either hate them or love them, but they cannot merely dismiss their presence, or their antics. The movie did not have any such luck. It was a complete flop.

The audience's lukewarm response to the first movie had been a major personal setback for me. By the time the second movie was being produced, I had understood that I could not afford to be attached to it. So the failure of the second movie did not come as that much of a shock. Its release and flop also marked the closure of an important chapter — my attempt at film making.

Now when I look back I find a couple of reasons why I failed at the art of movie-making. One of the reasons is that there are too many variables that go into the success or failure of a movie. Individual character performances and the ability of every crew member play a critical role. So do a host of external factors like distribution and exhibition, the kind of movies that are getting released at the same time, and the changing customer tastes. Probably I lost control of most of these factors that decide a movie's fate.

However, most people think of the film industry as disorganised. I think the film industry is anything but disorganised. Hundreds of professionals come together to make a single movie. They are all from different backgrounds, have different skill-sets and yet, they work towards a single objective for many months at a stretch — to try and make a success of something that is going to be approved or rejected by audiences in less than three hours. The process of bringing in so many different creative people to work together can never be a disorganised process, even if it may seem terribly chaotic.

I have a high regard for film production houses that manage to do multiple movies year after year. But I increasingly feel that in order to be successful at making movies, one has to be in a position where he or she can control the entire value chain — the production, post-production, distribution and exhibition. There are only a handful of people in the Indian film industry who manage to do this and not surprisingly, they are able to make a success out of most of the movies they produce.

The film industry has also undergone many changes in the last couple of years. The financial success of a big-banner movie is often sealed even before it is released. And the kind of movies that are being made has also changed, thanks largely to the emergence of multiplexes. The relatively affluent class that had stopped visiting the common theatres is now the prime audience for movies released at multiplexes. The movies that are being made reflect their life and their social setup. They are set in foreign locales and reflect their aspirations and insecurities.

If one considers India Two, they seem to have made their exit from the big screen of Hindi cinema. They are not included in the multiplex boom and they can no longer afford movie tickets at the newer theatres. More importantly, they cannot identify with many of the movies anymore. The disappearance of the 'angry young man' may have more to do with social change that our nation has gone through, but there are hardly any heroes or icons who the masses identify with. These days, India Two either watches movies on the cable television or at the video parlours. And once in a while a new trend takes over, like the sudden but short-lived popularity of Bhojpuri movies.

Yet, my fascination for popular Hindi movies hasn't subdued that much. There are only a few Hindi movies that I miss watching on the big screen. Family entertainment for us still means going out on a weekend and watching the latest Bollywood flick at the nearby multiplex or movie theatre.

Even though we do not make movies anymore, Hindi films play a crucial role in our business. They help us understand trends and changing customer preferences. And that includes identifying which modern retail formats will be successful in which cities and with which communities.

RAJAN MALHOTRA*

Kishoreji loves movies and is extremely passionate about them. It is a blessing for us that his first two movies didn't work. If they had, he would have been making movies and not opening retail stores. All our employees are very happy that he didn't stick to movies. But I am sure someday he will go back to them, simply because he believes that movies are the best communication medium. That will be

*Rajan Malhotra is Head, Big Bazaar. He joined the company in 2000.

the day when he is fully confident that he has unravelled the entertainment gene of the Indian masses. He still believes that he is a great marketer and someday he wants to weave a success story about film making as well.

Business @ the Speed of Thought

⚡

*'And, when you want something, all the universe
conspires in helping you to achieve it.'*

PAULO COELHO

I

Retail is a simple business. It is definitely much simpler than making movies and that's probably the reason why I fared better in retail, than in movies. At the very basics, retail is about buying and selling — something human beings have been doing since they started living in societies. All one needs, to be successful in retail, is common sense. Unfortunately, common sense is not that 'common.'

When we started off this business, none of us had any experience or any fancy degrees. All we had was lots of passion and a few common values that we cherished — simplicity, humility, willingness to learn and doing things the Indian way. Nothing was extraordinary about those of us who were part of the business in the initial stage. And whatever we have achieved is because the few ordinary people who got together, believed in the dream of achieving extraordinary things.

In August 2002, we launched the first Food Bazaar adjacent to Big Bazaar in High Street Phoenix, Mumbai. With this, the hypermarket format was complete and primed for expansion. By then we were managing twenty-eight large format stores covering 4 lakh square feet. It was clear that in order to grow the business further we needed a strong senior management team. The modern retail sector was still a small one and I knew most of the people in the sector personally. While there were definitely some talented people here, I realised that we also had to look at other sectors that had a similar customer interface. Along with people in the retail sector, we started to search for people in areas like telecom, consumer goods and consumer durables.

TORAL PATEL*

We started working actively with Pantaloon Retail around 2002, when the company was about to touch Rs 280 crore in turnover. The Big Bazaar format had met with initial success and the Pantaloon brand was well recognised and accepted.

Most entrepreneurs at this stage think about consolidation, but Kishore was well into implementing his audacious expansion plan. The biggest stumbling block an entrepreneur faces at this juncture is the ability to 'let go' and allow seasoned professionals to come in and drive expansion.

Kishore knew that he had to bring a quality senior management team, but was a bit hesitant about the kind of people he wanted. He would say, 'I don't want the fancy MBA-types. They don't fit in to our organisation because they are too proud of the fact that they are an MBA. *Suit, boot pahen ke baith jayenge par product nahi bikega.* (They will come in suits and ties but won't be able to sell the products).' He even told us that he didn't have a high opinion about consultants like us either. 'You consultants take my word and give it back to me.'

To Kishore, it was important to attract people who would fit the culture of the company. But finding such people wasn't easy. For one, retailing was a fairly nascent sector

---

*Toral Patel is a Senior Director at the executive search firm, Accord Group India. The company has worked closely with Pantaloon Retail in the hiring of the senior management team.

at the time. To make matters worse, Pantaloon Retail had a certain negative perception as an employer brand due to its entrepreneurial nature. Kishore hadn't bothered to hire a PR agency and was focussed on growth rather than on his or the company's image. Among his peers Kishore v as occasionally laughingly dismissed, ignored and was hardly ever invited for trade summits or trade body meetings. It was perceived to be a one-man show, a *bania* or *lala* company.

However, when we really started comparing it with other companies in the sector on parameters such as transparency, governance, involvement of promoters, scale, future plans and practices, Pantaloon surprisingly came out with flying colours. It was one of the two listed firms in this sector, and hence its financials were an open book. It had foreign and private equity investors who had completed due diligence on the company. It also had a successful model which was being expanded steadily. On the HR front, they had implemented some credible initiatives like Balanced Score Cards. Besides, once you heard out his plans, you came out believing that he could make it happen. We became the de facto HR-PR factory for Pantaloon. One of the first people I remember approaching back then was a professional in a competing retail chain. Even before we revealed the name of the company, he said that he liked his current job, and even if was planning to quit, he wouldn't join the 'likes of Pantaloon.' It took some painstaking industry research and forecasting, and many meetings to convince him to meet Kishore. Even after that, he took months before he finally took the plunge.

And that was pretty much the norm with most other candidates in those initial days.

It is true that not everyone can fit into our organisation. We have our own way of working and anyone who joins us, has to be prepared to unlearn certain things. The ideal people who form part of our organisation are those who are willing to go through the continuous process of learning, unlearning and relearning. Fortunately, most of those who joined us appreciated our beliefs, values and way of working.

For every senior person who comes into our organisation, I try to spend a good amount of time with him understanding his views, explaining our views and then attempt to bring them into agreement. Everyone else who joins, also goes through a similar process with his or her respective senior and mentor.

I believe that every human being has immense potential. As members of our organisational family, it became important for us to ensure that everyone who joins us understands the soul of the organisation, and that we help him achieve his true potential.

ANSHUMAN SINGH*

Meeting KB for an interview can be an unnerving experience. I had been warned by the person who had introduced us, not to get worried if he doesn't look into

---

*Anshuman Singh is the Chief Executive of the Value Fashion and Furnishing Division of Pantaloon Retail. He joined the company in 2001, quit it in 2005 and rejoined in 2006. During the intervening period he led Welspun India's foray into home furnishing retailing and served as its CEO (Domestic Division).

my eyes when he is speaking or if he doesn't seem to be paying much attention to me. Believe me, had that person not warned me, I would never ever have joined Pantaloon. KB by nature is a restless person and it is easily evident. Even during a meeting he will look at his computer screen, fidget with his mobile, take a few calls and it can be troubling for someone not used to it.

And if that is not enough, instead of asking me anything, he wanted me to ask him questions. 'Yes, tell me,' that's always his first sentence. When I enquired about my job profile, he said, 'We create jobs for particular people. We will create your job as per your profile. We find the people first and then find the job.' I think he still believes that. In fact, the first few months were pretty tough. I came from a very structured and hierarchical organisation. I was the youngest General Manager at Bombay Dyeing before I quit it and joined a relatively unknown company like Pantaloon. Within the first few days of joining, he told me that my style of thinking was very 'complicated.' That came as a rude shock to me and it took a lot of time for me to recover.

But slowly, while working with him one understands the power of simplicity. We managers tend to complicate matters with data, spreadsheets, charts, graphs, presentations, strategy sessions and all. KB has this ability to deconstruct everything and bring it down to the simple basics. He is also someone who needs to be understood well, before you engage with him. If he is asking whether something can be done, what he means is why don't you do it? He will speak a few words and provide a few dots on the broad picture which is in his mind. He would then expect you to chart your own course and follow it out. Possibilities are that you may not get what he wants during the early months. But once one gets to know his style, it becomes apparent that the best way to connect these dots is to look for the most simple and logical solutions. I can proudly claim that I know more about KB than most people. I was so fascinated by this man that during my first stint at Pantaloon, I kept studying him. He did not realise it, but I was a very, very diligent student of his. While setting up Welspun's retail business, I shamelessly copied everything I had learned from KB. And coming back to Pantaloon was like coming back to family.

It is quite obvious that for any organisation, it is very important to retain talented people, and so it was for us as well. The reason is not that as an organisation we are dependent on every colleague; but more because stable teams ensure speed and continuity. If we need speed, we need to retain our existing talent base. At the same time, we need to continuously attract talent so that we are able to grow at a faster pace. And for both of these, an organisation has to provide its people an environment in which they feel happy and motivated.

But it isn't an easy task to keep everyone happy in an organisation. Human beings by nature are unpredictable. Much like businesses, human beings go through their own ups and downs and every emotion, every interaction counts. While the pay-cheque and job satisfaction are important, I have often found that it is the way a person is perceived by others, that influences him to stay in or quit an organisation. How an individual's family, spouse, friends, peers feel about his job becomes a crucial deciding factor. Therefore, to make a person feel happy, one has to ensure that he or she feels a certain sense of pride and respect while working in an organisation.

Therefore, just like a company has to deal with its customers' emotions, it has to deal with every employee's emotions as well. However, I have found most management theories and tools focus only on how people can perform better, how a company can drive efficiency through more processes, etc. I feel that field of human resources till now has hardly dealt with how to manage human emotions and understand human dynamics. And unless a leader understands human dynamics, he can never get the best out of his colleagues.

SANJAY JOG*

Once one enters this office building for the first time, one notices the manifesto, the values, and the mission statement written all over the place. As one walks up to the second floor, scepticism sets in. One feels that these are too good to be true. The first reaction is that it must be a very pretentious kind of organisation. It's the typical feeling people get, and I too wasn't any different when I first walked in to meet Mr Biyani.

When I met him in his room, I expected him to ask me a set of questions. Instead, he started off with saying, 'Tell

---

*Sanjay Jog is the Head of Human Resources at Pantaloon Retail. He joined the company in 2005 and prior to this, he has been associated with Bharti Enterprises, RPG Group and Indian Hotels.

me what you want to know,' and then he stopped. I found that very strange as that wasn't how an interview was supposed to happen.

Yet, I asked him a couple of questions on business, his outlook, etc. Finally, I asked him why people in the company call him 'Kishoreji?' He asked me to explain what was wrong with 'Kishoreji?' I replied that nothing may be wrong but just that I found it strange. He then asked me what I call my elders in my family. I said, 'Well, we do add a *ji*.' So he said, 'Yes, it is the Indian way of calling someone with respect.' I argued saying that it sounds like 'Sethji.' He said, 'Yes it does, but you can call me anything else you want, I am okay with that.'

I was surprised and asked him, 'Isn't that carrying it too far?' He disagreed and our meeting ended there. It was very unconvincing and it took a fair amount of time and a few more meetings to convince myself that it was worth joining this organisation.

Later on, when one starts working with him, one tends to understand these nuances. For instance, we were having this discussion on what to offer as incentives to our store staff during Diwali. I was throwing up usual solutions like giving them cash rewards, or gifting them some bags, T-shirts, etc. But he had a completely different idea. He said, 'It's simple, what do we Indians like to do on Diwali? Paint our house.

'What happens, if we get our employees' houses painted and the clutter removed? Look at the benefits. The clutter is removed and his or her house is fresh. He or she comes to the store with a fresh mind. Their family feels proud about them. And the community that they live in will talk about how his or her company did this for them. It will create social recognition as well.'

That taught me a lot. This idea had everything that needs to go into an incentive: recognition, self-esteem, pride amongst family members and social recognition. It was a genuine way of earning the loyalty of our shop floor employees. And the idea was born out of the Indian way of doing things.

We now have a fairly strong senior management team. It is a fair mix of people who have grown from within the organisation as well as professionals who have served as chief executives and business heads at leading Indian and multinational companies. Quite a few of them have also been entrepreneurs at some time in their career. With the respect and recognition that we have gathered in the last few years, it has now definitely become far easier to attract senior professionals from other companies. But as an organisation we continue to depend much more on our colleagues at the shop floor than those working out of our offices.

Our colleagues at the shop floor are the ones who are in direct touch with the customers and therefore make or break our business. Most of them come from economically and socially backward sections of our society. And to understand their needs, aspirations and expectations is a completely different challenge that few companies in other sectors face.

For every new Big Bazaar that is opened, two hundred to three hundred people from surrounding localities get employed directly. The average age in our company is around twenty-seven years. But unlike many other companies, attrition is not a major issue for us. The challenge is to build self-confidence and pride in the minds of our colleagues who interact with the customers. They have to effectively engage with customers and help customers whenever required. Being present at the shop floor for long hours and being attentive to each customer's needs is both a physically and mentally demanding job. They need to know every detail about the products they sell, about the offers available in the store and explain these to all customers with a smile on their face, throughout the day.

The most crucial HR initiative that we undertake is Gurukool, a residential program that is attended by new employees who join our sales teams. This program exclusively focusses on self-development, grooming and building confidence. In addition, everyone is encouraged to pursue company-sponsored professional courses, including management courses at the institutes we have a tie-up with.

The potential of individuals to drive sales, make decisions at the blink of an eye and run businesses on their own is evident when one meets our store managers and their teams. In fact, the ideas behind some of our most successful consumer initiatives have come from our colleagues at the shop floor. Almost all our insights come from observing our customers at the stores, not from market research agencies. Every employee is trained to observe customer behaviour, is empowered to make decisions and take them forward. And at moments of crisis, like when a customer has fallen ill or in situations like riots, fire or floods, our colleagues at the shop floor have taken decisions that all of us are proud of.

Everyone in Mumbai will remember the flood on 26th July 2005. The city came to a standstill for almost three days. Offices and shops were shut down, Mumbai's lifeline, the train service was suspended and even newspapers were not printed. However, our Food Bazaar outlets that were not flooded remained open through the three days. Our colleagues at the store decided to stay back at the stores and keep them open. When the rains stopped, they called up customers and delivered milk and food items to their houses. None of these initiatives were suggested by the business heads at the head office. Store employees came together and rose up to the occasion. In the process they raised customers' expectations and proved that retail outlets are as much part of the urban infrastructure as the public transport system. It was our store colleagues who established through their own initiative that come rain or high water, our stores would continue to serve customers, and probably even better than on the usual days.

II

Retailers are prone to saying that in retail there are three things that are important — location, location and location. I may not go to that extent but it is a fact that in retail, real estate is a key factor and a good location does give a good head start. While more and more talented people today have taken on the reins to deliver growth across the organisation, a key enabler has been the real estate space that we have at our disposal.

We do not own most of the real estate spaces that we operate on. Our model is based on renting them out from developers and real estate owners on long-term agreements. While during the initial years of our business, there were hardly any shopping malls in the country, the scenario is clearly quite different today. However, most were not convinced about the potential of modern retail in the country even till a few years back. But we placed a bet on the future based on our direct experience of the growing consumerism in the country, and booked a considerable amount of retail space.

Rising real estate costs, especially in the metros, seem to be the single biggest impediment to the growth of this sector now. On the one hand, consumers have a lower disposable income to spend on shopping, since a large chunk of their income goes into servicing mortgages and home loans. On the other hand, high real estate prices increase the operational costs of running a large store. Ideally, real estate cost should be less than five percent of the total sales of a store in order to provide maximum benefit to customers. At the current rates, it can be as high as fifteen to twenty percent.

Fortunately, we do not pay such high rents because we secured our spaces much before other retailers joined in and before the prices shot through the roof. This foresight is now helping us deliver more value at a reasonable cost to our customers.

SANJAY CHANDRA*

We are about to open a new shopping mall in Noida that will be spread over 10 lakh square feet. But when we had started off we weren't sure whether India was ready for such a large mall and had planned for only 2 lakh square feet. Kishore was among the first few people who visited the spot and he gave us the confidence to scale up. His biggest strength is the pulse he has on the average Indian

---

*Sanjay Chandra is the Managing Director of Unitech Limited. Gurgaon based Unitech is among the fifty largest property companies in the world.

customer. It was because of his optimism and feedback that we scaled up the project five times and brought in eight anchor tenants.

Retail is an entrepreneur-led business. But in India, most retail companies are professionally run and often they are not able to take fast decisions. The professional CEO first goes to consultants or market research agencies to validate his choice and then goes to his owners for approval. The owners often do not know the ground reality. And the professionals are not empowered to take decisions and do not take bold steps.

Therefore, while most other retailers were, for instance, booking 40,000 square feet at a particular locality or town, Kishore would go ahead and book 1,00,000 square feet. In a moving real estate market, he is the one who therefore got the lowest prices and has been able to sign on more locations than anyone else. By getting in early, he has a far lower real estate cost structure and commands a much larger share of the retail real estate that is coming up.

Our experience has been that a retailer doesn't need to choose the most posh part of a city in order to be successful. Rather than the current profile of a locality, a retailer needs to look at the future potential of the locality. When we opened Big Bazaar in Lower Parel in Mumbai, at Hiland Park in Kolkata or at Koramangala in Bangalore, these were not the most attractive locations. However, these areas are undergoing steady development and our stores have benefited from the subsequent growth that has happened.

When it comes to choosing the right location we mostly rely on a lot of soft data and observations. We visit nearby markets, try to understand the kind of products that are available at the local *bazaars*, speak to people in the area and observe their shopping patterns. Rather than catchment analyses or consultant reports, often extremely unconventional tools have proved to be the best way to judge the potential of a particular city or locality.

For example, Bollywood and retail locations may seem to be completely unrelated on the surface. Yet, studying box office collections of different movies provides interesting clues on which format will be ideal for a particular town or location. Whether a movie like *Gadar* or *Dil Chhata Hai* did better, can give a retailer an idea of the demographic profile, tastes and preferences, and how open people are to change.

ANUJ PURI*

The first time I met Kishore, he said that he does a real estate transaction only when a bell rings in his head. I had no idea what he meant by 'a bell has to ring.' There would be properties which we thought were good, but if the bell didn't ring he would walk away within a couple of minutes. What made the bell ring, I haven't yet been able to decipher. But I did figure out, over time, that he is very sharp in identifying whether a property will be suitable for attracting customers. The famous 'bell' however has become a popular anecdote in our company.

One such early 'bell ringing' instance was about the High Street Phoenix property in Mumbai. We were working on behalf of the developers and I wasn't sure whether Kishore

---

*Anuj Puri is the Managing Director of Trammell Crow Meghraj, a leading international property consultancy firm.

would like the property. It was a textile mill land that was being converted into a mall. There were hutments all around it and Lower Parel in 2001 wasn't among the most preferred locations for any retailer. Kishore was planning to launch Big Bazaar in Mumbai and we had approached him with the hope that he would agree to be the first tenant at Phoenix. I felt that if at all he decided to take this property, it was quite obvious that he would choose the area facing the main road.

Kishore not only agreed to open the first Big Bazaar store over there, he even took a contrarian's call on the location he chose within the compound. Something he saw made him opt for an area *inside* the mill, over a more visible road-facing one. He looked at how a customer would come in, where the car park will be located, where she will get down and which will be the first store after the car park. And his choice was proved right when the mall became operational. Thereafter, we realised that the way Kishore judges a property is very different from the rest. He doesn't go by what anyone else says, he applies his own vision. Kishore can crystal gaze and see what it will be three to five years hence.

There is one more credit that is due to him. Thanks to Kishore, other retailers are now forced to take fast decisions when it comes to choosing a particular property. Earlier, it used to take a long time for retailers to decide on a property, often a month or two. But Kishore mostly takes a call on a property on the first visit itself. Therefore, others are now forced to decide on properties within two to three days!

Shopping malls in India are not just about shopping. Most urban centres in our country are starved of land and there are few public places where families can get together and spend quality time. Malls are slowly becoming part of the urban infrastructure where different communities come together not just to shop, but also to eat, get entertained and unwind. Therefore retailers and property developers have an opportunity to co-create the face of the new India that is emerging.

ATUL RUIA*

I first met Kishoreji when High Street Phoenix was being developed in 2001. By then, I had come to expect that CEOs would come with a team of six to ten people including some consultant. Discussions typically started with them telling us what all was wrong with the property, so that they could beat us down on the price. Kishoreji, on the other hand, came in alone at 9:30 in the morning. I took him to the site and within ten minutes, he said, 'I will take it.' It was a refreshing change from what I was encountering with other retailers. He had a very positive outlook and there was an immediate vibe between us.

In hindsight it seems he didn't come over to see the property. Knowing him, he must have checked it before. He had come over to understand whether a relationship could be built between us. I think a lot of Kishoreji's decisions are based on whether he thinks a relationship can be built.

---

*Atul Ruia is Director, Phoenix Mills Limited, the promoters of High Street Phoenix, Mumbai.

Our commercial agreement was finalised in two and a half minutes on a commercial flight. He had invited me to check the second Big Bazaar that was coming up in Hyderabad. On our way back on the flight, I suggested a price and he said yes to it and the deal was done. I had made up my mind at what price I will do the transaction and I quoted that figure. I didn't quote a higher figure and he knew it was a deal figure and it was over. Even today, most real estate developers don't quote an inflated figure. They know that Kishoreji isn't going to bargain, he is either going to say a yes or a no. I think many of the parameters that we put into that transaction, became the benchmark for a lot of other deals as well.

Kishoreji has often played the role of a mentor to me. He was quite insistent that High Street Phoenix should be developed as an inclusive environment where every citizen of Mumbai can come to relax, unwind and celebrate along with her family. He insisted that we do not charge for car parking, bring in both large and small retailers and even asked us not to throw the stray dogs out of the compound.

We work very closely with every developer with whom we are engaged. We share our own consumer understanding and insights and get involved, wherever required, in the design and management of the malls. Since 2001, we took a lead over other retailers in booking real estate space across most cities and towns in the country. By 2004, we had at our disposal a large bank of existing and upcoming real estate spaces across the country. We had also by then, built a strong senior management team.

At an organisational level, we were on a strong ground on the two crucial ingredients that go into retail — people and real estate. With Pantaloons, positioned in the lifestyle segment, and Big Bazaar, positioned in the value segment of the market, we had developed an extensive knowledge base about the Indian market and its consumers. We thought that it was an appropriate time for us to experiment with some new formats and product categories.

III

Around the turn of the century, an interesting trend was slowly becoming prominent in retailing across the globe. Department stores were slowly becoming less and less popular with customers. Large department stores offered a wide range of product categories — from apparel, luggage, toys, crockery, to home furnishing — as well as owned and managed the stock of products they sold inside the store and from their warehouses. These were referred to as the inventories of the retailer. Industry analysts started questioning whether this could still be the ideal retail model, and whether the changing retail environment marked the end of large department stores as we knew them.

On one side there were the speciality stores that focussed on a particular category — electronics, toys, women's wear or home appliances. Over the years, these had evolved into giant superstores and had become very popular with customers who went shopping for a particular product. On the other hand, there were discounters, hypermarkets and wholesale clubs that served the bargain-hunting customer very well. Department stores were squeezed in between and the new age shoppers found their ambience to be formal and boring.

To keep pace with these trends, some department stores were steadily reinventing themselves. The most prominent among them was UK based Selfridges chain. In 2003, Selfridges launched a new store in Birmingham, England that completely reinvented the idea of the department store. In stark contrast to the Selfridges store in London — featuring a long, grey, neoclassical façade dating back to 1909 — the new store in Birmingham had a post-modern architecture clad in aluminium and looked like something from outer space. As one walked into it, one realised that the grandeur and formality that characterised the older store had given way to a youthful and seamless character. Brands competed with each other within the store but there was no heirarchy of goods: watches competed with perfume, and luggage with fashion. In addition the store organised various shows, stunts and performances through the day and called it, 'shopping entertainment.'

Nearby in Bangkok, the famous Central store had a similar look and feel and was proving to be immensely popular with customers within the country and from abroad. Similar stores had come up in various parts of Southeast Asia, Japan and Europe. For customers, these new-age department stores seemed like a mall, just that they didn't have the walls that separate the different stores within a mall.

While this trend was becoming more and more apparent abroad, within India too, certain consumer patterns were emerging. Our experience showed that a customer visiting a mall typically walks into four or five stores. That includes a large store and a few smaller brand showrooms. After that fatigue sets in and he or she is unwilling to walk into any more stores at the mall.

So we asked ourselves, what would happen if we removed the walls between the different stores in a mall? In that case, a customer would be exposed to multiple brands at the same time, without the necessity of walking in and out of different stores. And along with shopping we could also provide her with other entertainment options. Customers could then enjoy a seamless shopping and entertainment experience.

Within the company itself there was a renewed confidence and an urge to play a larger role in shaping the modern retailing space in India. We had completed more than six years in retailing. With Big Bazaar we had tried and tested our skills at offering a wide range of categories while Pantaloons was firmly positioned in the lifestyle segment. We could now create shopping and entertainment landmarks in the cities in which we had already established a strong presence. Hardly any of the Indian cities had a 'destination mall' to attract customers from all nooks and corners of the city. As a leading retailer it was incumbent on us to take the lead and set up these destination malls in the country.

These three insights — the metamorphosis of department stores into developed markets; customer fatigue at the existing shopping malls in India; and the need to create destination malls in Indian cities — formed the genesis of the next format we started working on, Central. The objective was to create a retail format that was much larger and totally different from what India had seen till then. It would offer everything — from multiple brands for shopping, to restaurants, coffee shops, entertainment options and gaming zones — all under one roof. If we were able to deliver on these two fronts, we could attract customers from every part of the city and make it the city's prime shopping destination.

There were a couple of other issues that the Central model addressed quite well. Pantaloons outlets had limited space. We were positioning it as a fashion destination and the business model was based on selling mostly brands that we owned, or what are called private labels. However, with its increasing popularity, we were being approached by multiple foreign and Indian brands to stock these at Pantaloons. Central, being far bigger in size allowed us to open up a lot of space for other brands.

However, unlike in any other mall, these brands didn't pay us rent. Instead the brands paid us a certain percentage of their sales in the mall as commission. Based on the performance of these brands, we could decide on which to keep and which to discard. It also allowed us to provide a platform for smaller brands, especially in the ethnic wear category. As these brand owners owned the inventories or the stocks on their shelves, they were allowed to have some of their own people to man the store. Our focus areas were on building relationships with these brand owners, driving traffic inside the mall, managing it and providing customers with a complete bouquet of options for shopping, eating and entertainment.

The first Central mall was launched in Bangalore in May 2004. Measuring 1,20,000 square feet, it was spread over six floors and housed over three hundred brands in categories like apparel, footwear, accessories, home furnishing, music and books. In addition we had coffee shops, food courts, a Food Bazaar, restaurants, pubs and discotheques. A customer could also book tickets for movies and concerts, book travel tickets and make bill payments.

What has primarily made Central the 'destination mall' for Bangalore is its location. It is located in the heart of the city, at M.G. Road, where once Hotel Victoria stood. Moreover, we added a lot of features to further establish it as the focal point of the city. The Central Square located outside the mall building has been made available for art exhibitions, cultural performances, shows and product launches. And in 2005, the vintage car rally was flagged off from the Central flag-point, which has since become the epicentre for many such events. We also launched 'Radio Central' — India's first in-house retail radio station. Thus, Central captured in all its glory what we wanted a destination mall to be, and lived up to its tagline of 'Shop, Eat, and Celebrate.'

Soon after the launch of Bangalore Central, we opened the second Central in Hyderabad in November 2004. Once again it was located at the heart of the city on the Punjagutta Cross Road. Here, the roads connecting the city centre with Secunderabad, Jubilee Hills and the old part of the city, converge. It was more than double the size of Bangalore Central. Apart from over hundreds of brands to shop, it had food courts, restaurants, as well as a five-screen multiplex managed by PVR Cinemas. Much like the one in Bangalore, Hyderabad Central didn't take much time to become the nerve centre of the city. With an annual retail turnover of around Rs 200 crore it is presently among the largest retail destinations in the country.

With the success of the Central formats in Hyderabad and Bangalore, we started exploring how we could now take this format to every large city in India. We had been looking at Pune for a fairly long time. The city attracted a lot of students from across the country and therefore had a very young demographic profile. Moreover, what made it a perfect location for modern retail was the fact that the IT companies were setting up their base in the city and therefore more and more young working professionals were beginning to settle there. But since it lacked quality shopping malls and retail spaces at that time, we were forced to postpone our plans to launch Pantaloons and Big Bazaar in Pune.

With Central, we had the opportunity to create our own retail space that would suit the new set of consumers there. On a sunny morning in December 2005, everyone in our senior management team travelled to Pune and camped there. It was the beginning of a unique experiment in understanding a city whose demographic profile was entirely comprised of young professionals with whom we had never had any exclusive retailing experience. All of us were divided into four groups and each of these groups fanned out to different parts of the city. While some visited IT campuses, multiplexes, shopping malls and public parks, others spent their time at the small eateries, temples, movie theatres, regular college campuses and railway stations. For two days, each of these groups went around observing people, noticing their spending habits and taking pictures of people in various environments.

At the end of these two days, all of us came back to Mumbai and shared what we had learned and observed. This then formed the backdrop for our customer interface design for Pune Central. We opened Pune Central in April on the Bund Garden Road and it was larger than the one in Bangalore. A lot of minute detailing had gone into designing this mall. In retail, even a minor change in where a product is placed, or shifting it from one shelf to another, can increase or decrease its sales. Even to the extent of placement vis-à-vis the right or left hand of the customer when she is shopping can bring about a dramatic improvement in sales figures. At Pune Central, we took adequate care that no customer segment felt alienated inside the mall. There were dedicated places for senior citizens to sit and take rest, but the overall ambience of the mall exuded youthfulness and spirit.

College students are usually the most regular visitors of shopping malls. Many of them come in large groups to 'hang out together,' without necessarily making any purchases. In retailing parlance they are referred to as the 'mall rats.' At Pune Central we tried to ensure that everyone had something to attract them to spend money. Counters selling fashion accessories, fast food joints, coffee shops and a Pizza Hut outlet were thrown in to keep the young crowd engaged and to ensure that almost every footfall was monetised.

Central has turned out to be a unique concept that no other retailer has yet been able to replicate in India. It is a showcase of our skills at retailing. The latest Central opened in Vadodara — a city that is often ignored by many retailers but has a large consumption expenditure. Located in the Wadi Wadi area, Vadodara Central is spread across 1,50,000 square feet.

Managing such large retail spaces targeted at young consumers demands an obsession with creativity and newness. For every Central that we launched, we had to craft a unique and individual design. It was imperative for us to understand the customer profile of each city and most importantly, it required patience. Multiple variables had to be managed to ensure that a Central does not become yet another mall in the city. With its size and scale, its success entirely depended on whether or not it was able to become a *destination* mall in the city. We went through an intense learning experience and by now we have somewhat managed to crack the code for creating destination malls.

Central as a concept has now fully matured and we are now ready to launch Central outlets in all large cities in India. The concept leverages on the large retail real estate space we have at our disposal. In eleven large cities, along with our real estate partners we are developing large retail real estate spaces right in the centre of these cities for our Central outlets.

The largest of these outlets will come up in Kolkata. Located on the Lower Circular Road, it will be more than four times the size of Bangalore Central. For the upcoming Central malls, including the one in Kolkata, we have roped in Manhattan based Rockwell Group to design the malls. Rockwell Group is among the most prominent architectural design firms in the world. Best known for the design of the Kodak Theatre, where the Academy Awards are held, Rockwell has designed some of the finest shopping malls, airport complexes, restaurants, and spas in the US, Europe and Japan, as well as stage sets for Broadway musicals. With Rockwell as our design and architecture partners, we want to excel in designing the new landmarks of Indian cities.

IV

As we were working on building the Central model, we were also exploring how we could expand the number of brands that we owned. We realised that in order to attract a larger portion of the customer's wallet, we needed new formats and new retailing concepts.

In the months of January and February 2005, we acquired stakes in three small but strategic companies. The first one was Bangalore based Indus League Clothing. The company was founded by a group of former colleagues from Madura Graments. It had been funded by a clutch of private equity funds including ICICI Ventures from whom we bought the majority stake. The company had a very strong management team, a large manufacturing unit in Bangalore and, more importantly, two strong apparel brands, Indigo Nation and Scullers. With a fairly large retail network in place, we felt that we could provide these brands an ideal distribution platform to grow. These two large brands along with other brands could now get a larger national footprint piggybacking our retail chains. The success or failure of this strategy would provide us with insights on whether we could try similar models for growing other consumer brands through our own private equity fund.

The second company we acquired a stake in was Galaxy Entertainment. A listed company, Galaxy managed the popular Sports Bar, Brew Bar and Bowling Co. in Mumbai. It was therefore an interesting vehicle for us to understand the leisure and entertainment segment, where a large chunk of consumers' expenditure went.

The third company was Planet Sports, subsequently renamed Planet Retail. We picked up a forty-nine percent stake in the company. The remaining stake is held by a group based in Indonesia, owned by an entrepreneur of Indian origin, V.P. Sharma. Planet Retail operates a chain of stores called Planet Sports that sells sportswear and accessories of foreign brands like Wilson, Puma, Speedo and Converse. It also owns the exclusive Indian franchisee of international retailers like Marks & Spencer, Debenhams, Guess and Next. Apart from an opportunity to operate these international retailing brands in India, it allowed us to tap into a niche apparel segment like sportswear.

Along with these we started tapping into other niches as well. In 2005, we launched a new format named aLL, which stands for 'A Little Larger.' This targeted customers who wanted to buy plus-size garments, but couldn't find them in regular stores. It was a completely untapped market and these individuals mostly went to tailor shops to get their garments stitched. Some other of our early initiatives, Fashion Station — a value fashion chain — and

Gold Bazaar, to retail gold within Big Bazaar, didn't perform as well as we had expected. Two subsequent attempts at acquisition also fell through. We almost came close to acquiring a small home retail chain and a bookstore chain. In both the cases, the negotiations broke down at the last stage due to differences in opinion between the owners and us.

Both these failed attempts once again gave us the push to build new businesses on our own. The boom in housing was evident to everyone. A lot of consumption expenditure had started to go into buying new houses and renovating old ones. While it wasn't possible for us to build new houses and sell them to consumers, a significant part of the consumption spend could be tapped by retailing the products and services that are used for building and renovating houses.

In order to get into this market, we formed a new subsidiary company, Home Solutions Retail, in 2005. The flagship format of this company, Home Town, will be opening shortly in some of the larger cities in India. In the meantime, we have opened a number of smaller formats that will be exclusively selling electronics, consumer durables and furniture. These include, Collection i that caters to home furniture and furnishings, and EZone, that sells consumer durables and home electronics.

In 2006, we launched our books and music chain, Depot. It aims to provide, among other things, a non-intimidating environment that can attract a larger number of people into bookstores. One of its key initiatives is to tie up with publishers to reprint popular books in Indian languages and expand the market for this segment.

The Indian market is an extremely diverse and fragmented one and the mass market is essentially a 'mass of niches.' We realised the need to complement our large-format stores with a number of smaller speciality retailing formats to serve the different needs of Indian consumers. We are setting up multiple formats, from Chamosa — small kiosks that serve *chai* (tea) and *samosa* — to Home Town that will be a one-stop shop for every product and service that is required for home building and improvement.

Apart from our established formats like Big Bazaar, Pantaloons, Food Bazaar and Central, we have created two dozen formats that capture every need and aspiration of consumers. We now operate across ten lines of business — food; fashion and footwear; home solutions and consumer electronics; books and music; health, wellness and beauty; general merchandise; communication products; E-tailing; leisure and entertainment and financial products. In most of these businesses we operate at least two distinct formats — one for the value segment and the other for the lifestyle segment. The vision for us is to deliver everything, everywhere, to every Indian customer in the most profitable manner.

However, all the formats that we have launched till now have been developed keeping in mind the urban and semi-urban customers in India. But rural India accounts for fifty-five percent of the total private consumption and no retailer can afford to ignore the rural consumption market. But catering to customers in rural India has its own set of challenges.

There are 720 million consumers in rural India who live across 6,27,000 villages. Seventeen percent of these villages account for sixty percent of rural wealth. So even if a retailer aims for half of the rural opportunity, he has to be present in at least 1,00,000 villages. Most of these villages are separated by large distances and are relatively thinly populated. Therefore, the number of customers that a single retail outlet can attract in rural India is significantly low, making existing modern retail formats unviable.

For the past couple of years, we have been looking at how we can evolve a retailing format suited to the rural Indian context that is able to effectively capture rural consumption. Some of our senior management teams spent considerable amount of time travelling across villages, understanding their consumption patterns, and visiting *melas, haats* or fairs that are held there. The insights that we have gathered on the market conditions in the rural heartland, now form the basis for a new initiative that we are going to launch. It will be called KB's Wholesale Market.

Rather than reaching out to every rural consumer directly we are working on a partnership model with rural retailers. KB's Wholesale Market is being designed to act as a rural hub that will connect small manufacturers with small traders and retailers.

Today, a rural retailer has to travel long distances to cities and visit different wholesale markets to source the products he sells. There are a few clustered wholesalers and middle-men who dominate the wholesale market in semi-urban and rural India. Structural bottlenecks ensure that apart from the wholesalers, every other constituency — farmers, agri-producers, retailers and consumers are disadvantaged. Our studies show that there is a significant scope for increasing efficiency and building a transparent price discovery mechanism.

Spread over twenty-five to forty acres of land, KB's Wholesale Market will provide a large trading platform where a rural retailer can buy all his products from. It will also have cold and dry storage facilities, parking and transport facilities and public amenities. Hence, it will build a market for rural and agri-products and also create employment opportunities.

This model is still at a very nascent stage. While we have acquired land at two locations and are setting up the infrastructure for these hubs, it will take us quite some time to understand, fine-tune and further develop this model. It is hard to predict how this concept will evolve over a couple of months. We will have to go through a long phase of learning, but I believe it holds a lot of promise both for our organisation as well as the rural economy for the future.

V

As we were setting up multiple retail businesses, we realised that we needed to create a retail ecosystem that could keep pace with our growth. One of the biggest challenges we faced was with respect to real estate. While we had booked sufficient amount of real estate to build our retail formats, quite often we found that our growth was constrained by the delay in completion of the malls, by real estate developers. At times, we also found that the ambience and customer conveniences at the mall were not up to the standards that we had expected. Real estate costs were steadily going up and building sustainable retail businesses at existing costs was increasingly becoming difficult. And as retailers, we tend to have a better understanding of the customer than a real estate developer. While developers focus on maximising the rent per square feet, a retailer who occupies space in the mall wants to maximise the sales per square feet.

So, rather than complain about these issues, we decided to take on the responsibility and address them ourselves. In 2004, we started exploring the option of setting up our own malls. However, buying space and building malls and consumption centres is a capital-intensive business. Our retail business was not in a position to invest such large amounts in building malls. Therefore we started working on raising a real estate fund that could then invest in setting up malls. We became one of the first companies to raise one in 2005.

Shishir Baijal, who used to be the chief executive of Inox Leisure, a leading multiplex chain, joined us to lead the investment and management of this fund. Our real estate fund, Kshitij raised around $80 million from Indian investors that was then invested in developing malls across the country. The successful raising and deployment of the Kshitij fund formed the backdrop of our capital business.

SAMEER SAIN*

Future Capital Holdings (FCH) was conceived in the backseat of a Honda Accord, somewhere near Breach Candy, in Mumbai, in November 2005. Kishore and I had agreed on creating a private equity fund the previous month. However, as we continued our dialogue, it was apparent that Kishore had a greater ambition and I too had higher aspirations. I resigned from Goldman Sachs in January 2006 and FCH was officially born in February 2006. We already had a head start with an $80 million retail real estate fund (Kshitij) which Kishore moved into FCH along with a top notch team of thirty-five people lead by Shishir Baijal. FCH is now one year old, but I believe that it is a lot more advanced than its contemporaries. We divide its activities into three parts — ideas, investments and enterprises —

*Sameer Sain is the Managing Director of Future Capital Holdings. Prior to taking over this role, in January 2006, he served as a Managing Director in Goldman Sachs (Europe).

and have designed the organisation to be creative, free flowing and flat.

In addition to Kshitij, we now manage a $350 million real estate fund (Horizon), a $425 million private equity fund (Indivision), a $200 million Future Hotels fund and a couple of others are on their way. Most importantly, we have accumulated the finest talent in the shortest possible time in a highly competitive environment. We have hired people from financial conglomerates like Goldman Sachs, Blackstone, AIG, Ambit, ICICI Bank and consultancies like McKinsey, Boston Consulting, among others. We aspire that before Future Capital is five years old, it is considered the best financial services company.

A constant question that we have always asked ourselves is, how can we get an even larger share of our customers' wallet? The key to success in retailing is in getting customers to come back to your store again and again. With Pantaloons we made a small beginning, then came Big Bazaar, Food Bazaar, and Central, followed by many other formats that catered to almost every requirement of our customers. Yet, the question needed to be asked once again: how to induce more consumption?

It is a proven fact that consumption spending increases when customers have easier credit and financing options. We felt that we could further boost consumption at our stores if we could better our financing options. For buying a television or home furniture at our stores, many customers seek credit from banks. There was clearly an opportunity for us to address this need within our store.

In addition to its asset management business, Future Capital will now also be launching Money Market, a financial supermarket that will offer consumers loans and credit products to customers within our store. It will also offer investment products like mutual funds and insurance and thereby help us draw in a larger chunk of the consumption expenditure.

But facilitating consumption through access to money is not enough in the present scenario. A retailer has to create aspiration and the desire to consume. And this happens when the customer is exposed to brands that he or she identifies with.

In our fashion business, we had been reasonably successful in establishing our own brands or private labels. We had built these brands in a way that they reflected the tastes and ambitions of the new Indian consumers. We then started looking at how we could further extend our brand portfolio in other categories as well, like food, home care and consumer durables. A strong portfolio of brands helped us establish a stronger customer proposition and derive better margins from the business. A similar initiative was launched across our other businesses with the establishment of a new subsidiary, Future Brands.

SANTOSH DESAI*

In the past fifteen years there has been a paradigm shift in every segment of the Indian economy. New sectors have emerged, new lifestyles have evolved and new businesses have flourished. However, if one looks at the instances of consumer brands that have been created — one will see a dismal number. Very few organisations have

---

*Santosh Desai is CEO, Future Brands. In December 2006, he quit his role as CEO of McCann Erickson India to partner with the Future Group.

taken the initiative to create brands. And, most of the existing ones are extremely shallow in terms of a brand idea. Of the few strong brands that have come into prominence during this period, hardly any have been conceived in India. They seem to have been borrowed from the international market and therefore often lack a real connection with India.

However, during these years the desire among Indian consumers to communicate through the brands that they use has only gone up. They need brands as a device to articulate their new hopes, dreams and yearnings. But the new Indian is handicapped by the limited brand vocabulary that is available to him. The reason behind this is that marketers haven't been able to look at Indian consumers without preconceived notions. They have often taken an evolutionist approach — if the American economy or the Japanese economy was at a similar stage in the Sixties or Eighties as India is at today, they assume that consumers too would behave and aspire for products in a similar fashion. When the brands they launch do not succeed, they complain of low market penetration or lack of emerging categories.

Brands are a product of imagination. A brand is an idea and if translated properly, it can fire a customer's imagination. Therefore each brand needs to be developed on a fresh canvas. The Indian market is grossly underbranded and there is a lot of opportunity to conceive and create new brands that cater to Indian aspirations. While in retail one has to be extremely responsive to the everyday needs of the business, with brands one needs to take a more long-term view. In the long run, a strong set of brands can give our retail outlets a strong differentiator and increase their competitiveness. It can also drive the margins for the business. Eventually, Future Brands can strengthen the group's thought leadership in creating solutions, tailor-made for the Indian consumer.

Contrary to conventional logic, the most exciting opportunities today lie at the periphery of retail. Being in retail puts us in a unique position to attract and directly reach out to millions of customers who visit our stores every year. We are now in a position to leverage this asset and further strengthen our customer proposition and business models.

For customers, our presence across the consumption space means that they get the entire gamut of products and services at one location. More importantly, we can offer a strong platform to a lot of other companies to communicate with our customers. Of course, we will charge them for it, but that is going to help us keep our retail margins low and pass on more value to our customers. One of the ways to tap this opportunity is through retail media.

Retail media is a new concept in India, but has proved to be a very strong advertising and communication platform for brands across the world. It is based on the premise that it allows brands to communicate with customers when it matters the most — within the store, just before a customer is about to make a purchase decision.

Brands try to influence customer purchase decisions through advertisements in television, newspapers and magazines. Yet, customers make the final decision once they see the product. Whether they choose a particular brand of soap or pressure cooker over another is often decided within the store. Therefore the most effective and measurable way of reaching out to customers is through a media vehicle inside the store.

Retailers can offer brands to advertise on LCD screens placed within the store, points of sales (POS) displays, kiosks, hoardings inside and outside the store and even on radio channels played inside the store. Leading this initiative is Future Media, a subsidiary company that has started offering the retail media platform to brand owners and advertisers.

VI

I am often asked what is our core competency? Some companies make only cars, some make only steering wheels and some make only ball bearings, and most of them do a good job out of it. But how does a retailer sell insurance, run restaurants, manage private equity funds and charge brands for airing their advertisements on LCD screens within his store?

The notion of an organisation having a core competency in manufacturing a particular product is a legacy of the last century. It must have fitted in well at the time Henry Ford spoke about Model T, 'Any customer can have a car painted any colour that he wants as long as it is black.' It is a different world today where ideas and imagination drive organisations to success. The Indian economy today provides numerous opportunities in almost every business. The notion of core competency therefore, can no longer be defined in terms of a single product or service. It has to be defined in terms of knowledge, ideas and intangible assets.

Our core competency lies in understanding and delivering to Indian consumers. We won't make steel, neither will we build cars or set up large petrochemical complexes. But wherever there is a direct customer interface, we will try to capture some value in some form. Over the years, we have gained significant insights about the mind of the Indian consumer, a deep understanding of their emotions, needs and aspirations and how we can connect with each one of them. With this strong knowledge base, we think we are in the best position to capitalise the incredible consumption opportunities.

In order to firmly establish our presence across the entire consumption space, in 2006 we created Future Group — an umbrella entity that includes every initiative that we undertake. All our existing and new businesses are classified into six verticals: Retail, Capital, Brands, Media, Space and Logistics.

Possibly the biggest joy in life comes from shaping the future. The word 'future' for us signifies optimism, growth, achievement, strength and rewards. Future encourages us to explore areas yet unexplored; write rules yet unwritten; create new opportunities and build new success stories. Future Group is based on the belief that the future will be even brighter than what it is today. And our objective is to shape the future and make an enduring mark on the Indian consumption space of tomorrow.

However, it would have been foolish for us to assume that we can run and manage so many businesses entirely on our own. Therefore, through Future Group, we have created multiple platforms that help us bring in the knowledge and expertise of some of the best Indian and foreign companies, in each of these areas. Most of these initiatives are managed through separate and independent companies that bring in the expertise of our partners. This is complemented by our reach in the retailing space.

Through our real estate venture capital funds, we are investing in the development and management of more than fifty shopping malls across the country and these will come under the banner of Kshitij Retail Destinations. We are also developing market cities and consumption centres that will not just provide opportunities for shopping, but will also have commercial space for office complexes, hotels, entertainment zones and public spaces like parks and places of worship. To manage these properties, we have entered into a partnership with Singapore based CapitaLand, Asia's leading mall owner and manager.

A major initiative in the consumer finance space is going to be our insurance products that will be launched soon. We have formed joint venture companies for life and general insurance with Italian insurance major, Generali. Generali is among the largest insurance companies in the world, and brings in a wealth of expertise in selling insurance products both in Europe and Asia.

Other foreign companies we have joined hands with include French lingerie and women's wear maker Etam, UK based Lee Cooper and US based office stationery retailer, Staples. We have also partnered with Alpha Airports to set up shopping centres at the new international airports that are coming up across Indian cities.

Among the Indian companies we have partnered with are Talwalkar's, for setting up gyms and fitness centres in our newer malls; and Manipal Health Services with whom have teamed up to manage a pharmacy chain and a set of health clinics. Market leaders Gini & Jony and Liberty Shoes are helping us set up retail chains for children's apparel and footwear, respectively. We also have a joint venture with Blue Foods that owns restaurant brands like Copper Chimney, Noodle Bar, Cream Centre and Yatra.

I think we have till now merely scratched the surface of the possibilities latent in the Indian consumption space. There is a long way to go and I believe that the future lies in exploring the collaborative approach towards growth. I believe that based on the relationships we have built with different organisations, we can unlock a lot of value for our organisation and for our partners.

VII

The bedrock on which our organisation is built is relationships. Thousands of small and medium supply partners have helped us in every possible manner to deliver to our customers. We are also dependent on many of our colleagues to ensure that we continue to perform better every single day. As an organisation grows, it increasingly depends more and more on people and communities. Howsoever successful an individual or an organisation becomes, it has to count on innumerable people to grow and prosper.

It is the relationships that we have formed with our joint-venture partners, supply partners, business associates, investors and employees that help us move faster than many other organisations; and that will make us stay a step ahead of our competitors in the future. The relationships that we have nurtured and developed all these years are our biggest competitive asset.

At the heart of these relationships is a belief in creating win-win-win scenarios. I firmly believe that it is possible to create scenarios where we win, our business associates win, and our customers win. Once one approaches a business keeping this framework in mind, one sees mutual benefit in all human interactions.

However, creating win-win-wins is a tough task. The first step is to understand the other person's aspirations by seeing his or her point of view. The need to win is also there in people's mind: one needs to make the other person feel that he or she has won. So even if it means sacrificing something for the sake of building a relationship, it is generally a good start. In the long run, both the parties inevitably benefit from a relationship that has been built on a strong foundation.

Most businessmen make the mistake of creating an environment wherein only they win. They see life and business only as a competitive arena, not a cooperative one. They tend to think in dichotomies: strong or weak, hardball or softball, win or lose. But that kind of thinking doesn't help build long-lasting, helpful relationships. Relationships are built on principles, not on the basis of power and position.

I think the emphasis on building and nurturing relationships is a very Indian way of doing business. Unlike in the west, our society is based on values like humility and sharing. We are good at building relationships; it is something that comes naturally to us. But building and nurturing relationships is a hard-edged business driver that helps us operate our business with speed.

ANUJ PURI*

Kishore holds the belief that in every relationship there is always some measure of give and take. We work on behalf of real estate developers and whenever I have seen him interacting with a developer or owner of a property, I have noticed that he wants the other guy to win first. He doesn't like getting into a protracted negotiation, instead, he wants to build a long-term relationship. Even if the person quotes a slightly higher figure, he accepts

*Anuj Puri is the Managing Director of Trammell Crow Meghraj, a leading international property consultancy firm.

it, much to the surprise of others, including his own employees. Once when I questioned his magnanimity, he explained, 'If I am going to develop short-term relationships, most of my time will be spent on meeting new people and starting afresh with them.'

Of course, if the price is unreasonable, he immediately walks off, without getting into any discussion. But this belief in building relationships has given him an edge in most real estate deals. The market quotes Kishore a different price than what it quotes to other retailers. In his case, developers quote a realistic price, because they know if they quote an absurd figure, he will not get into a negotiation at all. At the same time, since he is not someone who brings down the price to the last rupee, he is often the first retailer a developer approaches with a new property.

Kishore now has a dedicated team that takes care of most of the property issues. He has given them a lot of authority and power to take big decisions. He has also ensured that this team has the required leeway to invest in a relationship, rather than just complete a transaction.

Even in a very cutthroat and competitive area like real estate I feel it is trust and honesty that drives business. I am a person with strong likes and dislikes. If I don't like somebody, I don't like somebody. Then everything about that person irritates me. And if there is one thing that I can't stand, it is dishonesty. I deal honestly in every transaction and expect the same from business partners. With most real estate developers in the country, we have been fortunate enough to build long-term relationships that have lasted beyond just one or two transactions.

To me, relationships are very similar to arranged marriages in India. In arranged marriages, both the families invest a lot of time to understand each other and see whether the family values match. The marriage is finalised only after both the families feel comfortable. The love between the bride and the groom actually develops post-marriage.

In relationships too, it is very important to understand the person or the organisation before getting into a transaction. It takes time for a certain amount of trust to develop. And when there is trust, one doesn't need to get into the details of every transaction. With trust, one can assume that in every transaction, the best interests of both the parties will be looked after.

MANISH KALANI*

When Kishoreji visited our mall for the first time, it was under construction. He had done a transaction with my cousin, Atul Ruia who then introduced us. Our discussion lasted for thirty minutes and he made some strong observations about where we were going wrong with the mall. He then headed for Pakeeza, a large store that is popular in Indore. There he noticed that Pakeeza reimbursed the rickshaw fares of customers who visited the store in the afternoon. He came back all excited about the idea of incentivising customers to shop during low-business hours. For some time, the Big Bazaar at Phoenix too reimburses customers' cab fares. That somehow

---

*Manish Kalani is the developer of the Treasure Island mall in Indore. He is also the Managing Director of Kalani Industries.

generated a lot of respect for the man. It proved to me that he was not just giving advice to others, he himself was open to learn from anyone and everyone.

Few months later we met at the Taj Hotel in Mumbai — KB, Atul and myself. He took a Taj pad, and put in four points: terms, escalation, rate and infrastructure. He jotted down some notes under each, but left the most important one, 'rate,' blank. He then signed on it and that became the terms sheet. Before leaving he said, 'Atul, you fix up the rate. I trust Atul to be fair. It should be a workable deal.' It left the both of us surprised and the meeting had ended in exactly seven minutes.

The first step in building trust is to have a positive frame of mind. One has to be an optimist in life and believe in people. As the saying goes, 'Trust begets trust.' The only way one can make a man trustworthy is by trusting him. In all good relationships, including those with partners, friends and family, the most important ingredient is mutual trust.

From my own experience I can say that placement of trust in people has allowed us to achieve what otherwise would have been impossible. Trust in a person makes him go an extra mile to help you in times of your need. There have also been times when I felt betrayed by people. But the benefits that I have got from trusting people far outweigh the occasional setbacks.

Time and again, I have tried to underscore the importance of trust within our organisation. I think it is very important for all of us to learn about trust, how it works and how to build it. Once again, it is all about human dynamics.

At the very basics, trust is an emotion that keeps people together. It can also have very real financial implications — when trust suffers, so does speed and productivity.

SONIA MANCHANDA*

Recently, we were working with a typical old economy company and the lady there would sound paranoid whenever we met her. She would say things like, 'Please close the door, please don't tell anyone about what you are doing, our competition copies us.' And the reason they get into a situation is because they are damn slow. On the other hand, our work with Pantaloon is completely open and we haven't signed a single client confidentiality agreement till date. The best part about working with Kishoreji is that he can recognise a good idea, and he will get it done the moment you show it to him. There will be absolutely no waste of time. He can be really rude and completely rubbish an idea or he can come up with something like, 'This is the best design idea in the world!' He speaks in these superlatives and once he gets excited about something, he is completely taken up by it. It's a childlike quality and his impatience and restlessness ensure that things move.

Initially, I used to be taken aback by his strong responses. Over time I realised that with so much work, he didn't

---

*Sonia Manchanda is a co-founder of Bangalore based Idiom Design & Consultancy. She has worked with Pantaloon Retail on the customer interaction strategy for almost a decade.

really have the time to indulge someone. He isn't a person who gets into any kind of sweet talk. He is frank and upfront with his opinions and has his own way of winning over people. We are all family to him. He doesn't have to say these things, we just know them.

The Pantaloon Way

'Where the mind is without fear and the head is held high;
Where knowledge is free... Into that heaven of freedom,
my Father, let my country awake.'

RABINDRANATH TAGORE

I

At most companies, whether it is in India or abroad, one notices people working within hierarchies; decision-making being dominated by systems and processes; and the way water-tight structures define how every initiative should be undertaken. Everything is discussed and analysed threadbare and there is a need for perfection at every step.

Our business had none of these characteristics. We were a fluid organisation, where anyone could take on a new responsibility and execute it the way they wanted. We got into new areas in the hope that we will learn on the way and evolve as we go along. So whenever I met someone who had come in touch with our company, I would hear a long list of criticism. Most found us to be unstructured, and quite chaotic. To outsiders, our business decisions seemed to be based more on intuition and gut-feel, rather than on any hardcore analysis or research. They typically felt there was a complete lack of procedure in the way we approached our business.

For some time, it left me confused. The criticisms seemed to have some truth in them. Yet, each of these 'troubling' attributes had worked for us. As I started to introspect and understand each of these issues, I noticed a pattern.

Most business organisations are dominated by engineers, B-school graduates and chartered accountants. They are all trained to be analytical and logical in everything they do. Essentially, this is the way our left-brain works. This part of the brain is verbal and processes information in an analytical and sequential way, looking first at the pieces then putting them together to get the whole.

The right-side of the brain is the creative or visual part. It helps process information in an intuitive and simultaneous way, looking first at the whole picture, then the details. Depending on one's upbringing and formal education, one side of the brain dominates over the other.

I found this a useful way to understand and interpret human and organisational behaviour. I also felt that for a business to grow and flourish, one needed to use both sides of the brain, or both the approaches — the analytical and the creative. An organisation dominated by systems, analyses and processes, will only be good at repeatedly performing one particular task very well. But it wouldn't be able to innovate or create something really new. On the other hand, creativity alone can not drive business. Discipline is required to make businesses work efficiently. The happy solution is the marriage of both these aspects.

Coincidentally, while we were studying these factors closely, a new way of approaching business management was slowly gaining popularity in many respected companies. It went by the name of 'design management.' A lot of companies, including Procter & Gamble and GE, were talking about the need to bring about design-led thinking and creativity into business. The leading universities in the United States were introducing courses on creativity in their business curriculum. Stanford University set up a D-School or design school where its graduates from the engineering and business schools could learn about design.

Conventionally, design was associated only with product or industrial design. Industrial products and graphics are outcomes of the design process, but proponents of design management suggested that these do not define the boundaries of design-led thinking any longer. Communication, customer experience, logistics, organisation structures and even strategy can be tangible outcomes of design-led thinking. Design management, as many of them suggested, can be the most effective tool for applied innovation.

When we started to understand this area, we realised that this was something we easily identified with. We also felt that learning more about design management could help us formalise our way of working and bring in even more creativity and innovation into our organisation.

Being in the business of fashion, design had always been a key function within our organisation. Moreover, we had consistently emphasised on observing customers and then evolving solutions for them. This also happens to be the same process with which successful designers work. While designing a product, designers take an empathetic view of the customer or the user of the product. They understand how the user will interact with the product and how that interface can be improved. Sometime towards the end of 2004, we decided to take design out of the exclusive domain of fashion designers and put it in a holistic context where it would also impact our organisational dynamics. We looked at the multiple manifestations that design can have, and we found that it was far too important to be left to designers alone.

So how did we define design? We said that design is not just about aesthetics or prettifying things. Design is a user-focussed, prototype-based development tool that can make our organisation adapt to the fast-changing external environment. Building a design-led organisation requires creativity, a deep understanding and empathy of human behaviour. It also requires the skill to synthesise different and often conflicting trends and ideas.

The subject of design is not something that is alien or very difficult to understand. Design comes naturally to human beings —

we often use creativity and design in our daily interaction with others. In business, design revolves around understanding customers and users. Retailing is completely a customer-led business and design management helps us bring the customer at the very centre of the decision-making process. Whether it is in finance, technology, human resources or corporate planning, every function needs to think 'customer-first.' Design-led thinking can help organisations achieve that and ultimately lead to better financial performance.

DARLIE O. KOSHY*

In a business, the human capital and the creative capital are as important as the financial capital. And it is possible to envelope each of these through design thinking and designing as a process. Design is a creative activity where logic and intuition interact to develop opportunities, initiate desirable changes and facilitate innovations. Design is about connecting the dots that initially seem to be entirely unrelated. Synthesis is the key. Design can move horizontally across all segments of industry, commerce and development. Business leaders who appreciate this can discover how design makes a difference to almost all aspects of business. In retailing, everything is determined by customers and customers are heavily influenced by design. That's because design connects with their emotions

*Dr Darlie O. Koshy is Director, National Institute of Design (NID), Ahmedabad. He is also an Independent Director on the board of Pantaloon Retail.

and feelings. Therefore design has to be at the core of retailing.

I also believe that a strategy can be successful only when it goes through constant adjustment, innovation and creativity. Professionals involved in developing strategy need to view an organisation as an unfinished prototype. We live in an imperfect world, and it is meaningless to strive for perfection. It is far better to strive for excellence. Strategy therefore needs to continously respond and adapt to the changing external environment. It has to be a continuous process of evolution and improvement.

Prototyping has played an extremely crucial role in everything we have attempted. Most outsiders admire or dislike us for one basic thing — the frequency with which we launched new businesses or developed new formats. Few realised that behind these risks were two simple rules that we followed. One was to always have a backup plan ready. Most of the time we did not know whether an initiative would succeed, but if things went wrong, we knew we could cut our losses fast and move on to the backup plan. The other rule was prototyping. Every initiative, every concept or format we launched, always went through a prototype phase. We built it on a small scale and opened it to a customer interface. We then watched and learnt from how customers reacted to it, before we scaled it up. Any initiative at our organisation, howsoever big or small it is, must follow these two rules.

Design thinking is inherently a prototyping process. Once a promising idea has been spotted, one can build on it with drawings, models, stories or even a film that would describe a product, system, or service. The aim during this phase is to elicit feedback, before it is taken outside the organisation and exposed to a small set of customers. These models are not expected to be perfect. Instead, they need to go through constant adjustment and improvements based on suggestions and feedback. When one rapidly prototypes in this way, one actually begins to build the strategy. This process then allows an organisation to unlock one of its most valuable assets: people's intuitions.

Design processes are basically about this trial and error wherein one observes the world, identifies patterns of behaviour, generates ideas, gets feedback, repeats the process, and keeps refining. Essentially, design is about creation and destruction. A good designer constantly innovates, creates and then destroys to create something even better once again.

In our organisation, strategy documents are often pictorial by nature; they have images and concepts, rather than just text and graphs. Instead of following the regular presentation format, our strategy documents often tell stories that help our managers emotionally experience and connect the strategy to real life.

I have also found, contrary to typical management wisdom, some amount of chaos and ambiguity can play a significant role in the development of strategy. We live in a complex world and I keep hearing managers complaining about the absence of a level playing field, about uncertain business environments. Most business and economic theories are built on the delusive assumption, which I have never been able to appreciate, 'ceteris paribus' or 'all else being equal.' Business, unfortunately, is not about 'all else being equal' and as an entrepreneur one cannot complain that things are not available on a silver platter. I think we Indians are especially good at managing uncertain situations — very few things are certain in our lives, be it the electricity connection, water supply or traffic convenience.

Therefore, in a fast changing environment, where everything is fluid and chaotic, the strategic plan of an organisation cannot be written on stone. Long-term objectives and goals have to be set, but the road map needs to be an evolving one. It is like playing football — you know where the goalpost is, but you can't draw up a detailed plan to score a goal. You can't predict how the opponent team will play, which teammate might get injured or how the pitch will turn out. A footballer has to be agile and alert *on the field* — there is just no other way, even if he is playing by a strategy.

The success of an organisation depends on its ability to adapt and innovate when faced with a roadblock. A minutely detailed road map is only a preparation for a rude shock. Moreover, I like to keep everybody guessing. I don't want our competitors to predict our game plan. And even with colleagues, a little bit of uncertainty enables them to tackle sudden or even disruptive changes in a much better manner. In such scenarios, the same ambiguity and chaos that disables many managers stimulates those who believe in design-led thinking. Design-led thinking works even when there is lack of sufficient information or enough options. It helps people innovate and take new initiatives, rather than just follow a set path.

But creating a design-led organisation is easier said than done. Design is a collaborative process and requires multi-disciplinary teams to come together and share their inputs and insights. We have been introducing people from varied educational and professional backgrounds into our design process. Apart from designers, there are economists, ethnographers and sociologists working across our teams. They learn from engineers, management graduates and chartered accountants and pass on their learning to the others in the team. Professionals from diverse backgrounds bring in new thoughts and solutions to address challenges. Most of our senior and middle management teams have gone through extensive design-thinking workshops with these people. While we have made a beginning, we still remain far from being a fully design-led company.

A significant development in institutionalising design-thinking in our strategy was the creation of Idiom, an independent design and consultancy firm, based in Bangalore. In terms of scale and quality of work it will one day become comparable to the San Francisco based design powerhouse, IDEO, which is leading innovation in design in the world today. Personally speaking, Idiom has been one of the finest creations I have been involved in.

II

Joseph Chemmanur Hall is located in Bangalore's Indiranagar locality. It was constructed by the local church as an auditorium complex. It is now home to the largest design group in India, Idiom. A team of over a hundred and eighty designers from multiple disciplines work out of the auditorium that has now been converted into an open workplace. Every small and big idea related to our customer interface is debated, discussed, prototyped and given shape at Idiom.

One of the main reasons why we have been able to undertake so many initiatives across the consumption space has been the creation of Idiom. In a span of eighteen months since it was founded, Idiom has become the think-tank for our organisation and incubator of ideas and innovation within the company.

The 180-member team at Idiom works in a highly experiential manner. We don't expect big ideas to come from sitting in bland conference rooms. Instead, these team members spend a good amount of time out in the streets as active observers and passive bystanders. Idiom doesn't appoint market research agencies to understand customers. Instead, the team members blend into crowds, watch and observe them. When they return to the auditorium, they have notes, photographs and recordings of what they have seen or heard. The aim is to get social, economic, cultural and psychological insights rather than just numbers. If you walk into the auditorium, you will see the walls plastered with images, diagrams, flowcharts and photographs.

The entire team at Idiom is engaged in collective idea-making. The multi-disciplinary thinking that gets integrated into one single design is amazing. Idiom follows a simple eight-step process to identify a winning idea that can be implemented fast. We also pass on ideas we have generated within the company to Idiom. Idiom incubates the ideas for some time, develops insights and then expands on them. Be it on home, fashion, books, communications, leisure, entertainment or any of our businesses, Idiom combines intuition, observation and experience to come up with innovative solutions for customers. Since they work independently of our company, they are able to generate richer, stronger ideas that are hardwired to the marketplace.

Creating such an entity was no cakewalk. While setting up Pantaloons and Big Bazaar we had been working with two design firms, Tessaract and Esign. Esign, led by Sonia Manchanda, was a small and successful firm handling strategic and communication design projects. Tessaract, led by Jacob, Sunder and Anand, was a more experienced firm and had been working on product, furniture and space design for a lot of retail companies. Put together, they had around thirty designers, mostly graduates from National Institute of Design (NID). We had a long relationship with both of these firms because they complemented each other's design strengths and were able to provide a complete solution to our design needs.

As we started to expand both in scale and in the number of formats, I encouraged these two teams to come together and form a design powerhouse. However, being creative people, they wanted to be independent. They didn't want to be part of a corporate group. For three years I tried to get them together and spent many days and nights with their teams allaying their fears and motivating them to join hands and grow.

JACOB MATHEW*

The genesis of Idiom can be traced back to the Mumbai-Pune expressway. Once, while we were driving out of Mumbai, we reached a point where we were completely lost — we just couldn't locate the expressway entry point. We went round and round in circles and there wasn't any signage to help us out. Kishoreji suddenly started mumbling, 'You NID people. It's thirty years since the institute was set up and there is no sign of you guys.' I was taken aback. I tried to point out to him all the good work that NID graduates had done, designing the logo for State Bank of India, for Indian Airlines and for numerous

---

*Jacob Mathew is one of the co-founders of Bangalore based Idiom Design & Consulting. He has been associated in the design, layout and positioning strategy for most formats of Pantaloon Retail.

Indian companies. He shot back asking me to name some good design groups. I named some of them, but he would just rubbish them saying that they are too small to make any significant impact.

He had been quick to recognise the potential of design. The idea and versatility of what design could do was quite clear to him. We were developing his entire customer interface across most formats. But now he was set to scale up very fast across multiple formats and he wanted us to keep pace with him.

When he first told us about merging Esign and Tesseract, we didn't respond. Designers have a very boutique mentality. We discussed it amongst ourselves, but it's not easy to get a bunch of designers to work together. Design, we said was organic and fluid, and that's how we thought our organisation should be. Kishoreji's perpetual complain was that we tend to think very small. He would pass remarks such as, 'You NID people think small. You guys have the potential but...'

But what all of us, in both the organisations wanted, was a reassurance that we could work independently. We were small setups and we wanted to remain that way, we didn't want to be part of a huge company and get lost in the process. A couple of other companies were willing to fund us, but they wanted us to be part of their groups.

But then Kishoreji was someone in whom we had implicit trust. He is a man of dreams and his ideas are often very infectious. So we debated amongst ourselves for some time and whenever we were in Mumbai we would get into long sessions with him. It must have been tough for him, but he was committed to it. He even spoke to our team members individually. We could see that he was putting in a lot of effort.

Finally, in April 2005, Idiom was formed with the merger of Tesseract and Esign. I became the mentor of the company.

Within such a short period, Idiom has grown more than five times in size and in terms of people. While Idiom does a lot of work for our group companies, they have a long list of clients with whom they have developed steady relationships. Some of these include Godrej's retail initiative Aaadhar, Infosys, Royal Orchid hotels, WorldSpace, Tata Telecom and other large setups.

Idiom works across all facets of design, from product and industrial design to communication and branding, design of space, stores and interiors. It plays a major role in building our consumer strategy. Considering the amount of work that Idiom has done for us, I can't imagine any other firm in the world that can do a similar job at this cost. It takes a lot of time to generate ideas, develop them, prototype them and implement them and Idiom is helping us do all these multiple things at a high speed. Idiom works independently of Future Group and yet in many ways institutionalises the process of innovation within our organisation.

I believe Idiom has the potential to become the best design company in the world. It is a chance and it may be too early to say, but Idiom definitely has the capacity to make it. Most importantly, Idiom has been successful in incorporating Indian-ness into their design; and they can now influence many things in India.

GIRISH RAJ*

While setting up Idiom, we thought that if there is a global idiom of design, there could also be an Indian idiom of design. Management or design education is very international and most of what we learn is very western. The western way of design is about look and feel, and design is used as a means to prove superiority over the rest. It establishes things like '*mine* is better than yours, bigger than yours or more high-tech than yours.'

Indian culture however never encourages reductiveness or exclusivity. I think the Indian way of design is integrative and inclusive. It brings together various facets of our culture that may often seem to be mutually conflicting. In India, one can't look at the highest common factor — one has to work from the lowest common denominator. Most of the communication or branding in India does not take the general public into account. Nine out of ten Indians think in their vernacular language, yet most of the professionals in the consumer business are convent-educated, English-speaking people. These were some of the things we had realised and we found in KB a person who also believed in them.

Innovation is about creating change, not reacting to change. No one has seen the future and no one can define it in black and white. The future is a fluid entity that an organisation imagines

---

*Girish Raj is one of the co-founders of Bangalore based Idiom Design & Consulting.

and creates. Design-led thinking will help in generating desirable future scenarios for us. Complementing it are tools like storytelling, memetics and the idea of going with the flow.

III

Human beings are wont to learn by imitation and often copy each other's behaviours — from adolescents taking to smoking, to adults playing games on their cellphones. Family, community and the society at large influences human beings to behave the way they do.

Take for instance one of my friends, Srikrishna. Srikrishna's father was born and brought up in a small village and never tasted wheat or any other staple. He was a hundred percent rice eater. Srikrishna too prefers to have rice in most of his meals, though he doesn't mind eating wheat or corn when he is eating out. But seventy percent of his meals are rice-based. His rice eating habit, grown out of the community he grew up in, has now been influenced by fast food chains, Italian restaurants and the recipes his wife takes down from television.

Under these circumstances, what may be interesting to study is how Srikrishna's son's eating habit is developing. And the answer may lie in understanding memes. Memes are essentially the cultural equivalent of a gene. They replicate cultural information that is transmitted from person to person, much like genes transmit hereditary information from a person to his or her progeny. In the case of Srikrishna's son, the question that needs to be asked is whether he will be influenced by the external culture and end up consuming more non-rice foods? Or will his Kannadiga cultural gene hold strong and force him to prefer rice over any other staple? What factors will affect and determine his rice eating habit? Essentially, what will be the extent of change in the next generation of rice eaters and how do we need to evolve before the customer does?

A meme can be anything, an image that gets easily replicated in the mass media and public consciousness, a particular taste or pattern of behaviour, a catchphrase that rolls off your tongue and sticks in your mind, or a tune, an idea, a fashion trend or even a new movie. Like a gene, memes synthesise complex information, concepts and ideas and pass them along with little effort.

The study of memes is called memetics. It is a mixture of learning from genetics, psychology, anthropology and other social sciences that are put together for the behavioural context. The term 'meme' was coined in Richard Dawkins' book, *The Selfish Gene*. Though a hotly debated subject, we are increasingly finding memetics to be an interesting tool to understand, predict and influence trends in society. Till now, memetics has been mostly used for viral marketing. But we feel that there is ample scope to use memes to understand changing socio-economic and cultural trends.

Memetics can be used to interpret these trends and then influence consumers. For example, one can go back to the origins of fashion to understand why women in the northern parts of the country pierce the left side of their nose whereas women in the south pierce their right. Or how is the sari as a dress and fashion statement changing?

Memes, as a fundamental property, evolve via natural selection through replication, mutation, survival and competition. For example, while one idea may become extinct, other ideas survive, spread and mutate, after modification.

Academics suggest that a successful meme has three qualities: fecundity (it should be easy to replicate), fidelity (copies of it should be accurate) and longevity (it should have a long life). Designing products and services based on the understanding of memetics may well launch a revolution in marketing strategy. These products can simply be promoted through the natural energy of our target groups — by word-of-mouth.

For example, a garment manufacturer may want to know if there is a demand for shirts with transparent pockets so that people can flaunt their mobile phones. Or do people want multi-utility garments that can quickly and deceptively be changed from office-wear to party-wear? And if there is a demand, how does a retailer convert it into a winning business proposition?

Internally, our teams working on understanding and interpreting memes have come up with interesting ideas by identifying the emerging memes in India. From shoes with adjustable soles that can increase or decrease your height, to T-shirts that will come with Velcro appliqués or alphabets, so that you can make and change the graphics on your shirt; we are looking at innovative products that can capitalise on the emerging memes in the Indian consumption sector.

Memetics has become an important tool for us because it brings the understanding of culture and human behaviour at the centre stage of developing business strategy. We haven't yet captured the full potential of memetics and figured out how best to leverage it. It is still an early attempt to make sense of our country's diversity and engage with it.

IV

The trick, according to Chiang, was for Jonathan to stop seeing himself as trapped inside a limited body that had a forty-two inch wingspan

*and performance that could be plotted on a chart. The trick was to know
that his true nature lived, as perfect as an unwritten number, everywhere
at once across space and time.*

Those who recognise this excerpt will be familiar with the story
Jonathan Livingston Seagull by Richard Bach. It is the simple story
of a seagull, Jonathan, who defies convention and decides to learn
to fly higher than his flock. Jonathan refuses to listen to his folks
and tries to go where no other seagulls have gone. Against all
odds, he pursues his single-minded objective. In the latter part
of the story, he meets Chiang who encourages Jonathan to think
against the tide and redefine his capabilities.

Jonathan's devotion and willingness to learn help him overcome
all odds in flying much higher and much faster than any other
seagull. When we adapted this story and compared it to what we
had attempted in our organisation, the basic characteristics and
lessons of the story seemed similar. We combined it with visuals,
blurbs and images, and it became a powerful tool to engage and
communicate our strategy, not only to our employees but even
to outsiders. Storytelling has now become an important tool for
us to develop and communicate strategy.

We have adapted numerous stories, from Paulo Coelho's *The
Alchemist* to Bollywood flicks, to suit our specific need and context.
While a session on how to face competition may involve a story
based on a common man's interface with various companies, a
vendor management strategy document can well evolve from a
story about a small entrepreneur from a nondescript town, who
visits the city and finds a partner in us, who will help to build and
grow his business. New employees are introduced to our strategy
and background through various storytelling sessions and are then

encouraged to develop their own stories based on what they have learnt till that time. A story helps create an understanding that goes beyond just the financial numbers and captures the values, thought process and the soul of our organisation.

We keep our storytelling sessions simple and interactive. An ideal story should have few characters, a sense of humour and intrigue, a twist in the tale and a promising end. Rather than relying on words alone, we found the pictorial mode of storytelling to be more engaging and versatile. Images, blurbs and different colours are weaved into the basic theme of the story so it can be understood by everyone and make an emotional connection. People need to have a visceral understanding — an image in their minds — of why we have chosen a certain strategy and what we are attempting to create with it. Storytelling does that in the most effective way.

It is remarkable how often business strategy, the purpose of which is to direct action towards a desired outcome, leads to just the opposite: stagnation. The reason for this is that the tools which executives traditionally use to communicate strategy — spreadsheets and PowerPoint decks — convey a narrow and often misleading picture of the organisation.

On the other hand, storytelling is the oldest art of communication. Since time immemorial, and across all civilisations, human beings have used stories to pass on culture, learning, knowledge and values from one generation to another. Yet, modern-day business organisations fail to appreciate the most natural way of conveying ideas.

Along with storytelling, what has played a key role in evolving our strategy is scenario planning. As a tool, scenario planning is mostly used in the energy sector and is often based on mathematical models and analytics. However, in our organisation scenario planning is based more on intuition and imagination than on drawing from established models. We know that we cannot extrapolate from the past to envision the future. There can be no comparison of what is currently happening in India, in the retailing sector, with what happened in the Sixties in the US or in the Nineties in Southeast Asia. Insights from those eras and settings cannot be applied to the Indian context. With the pace at which India is growing and changing, it is unreasonable to use an approach that worked somewhere else and expect it to succeed here. Therefore, one needs to look at the future, without being prejudiced by the past.

Scenario planning builds upon the original entrepreneurial power of creative foresight. We build on hypothetical market scenarios and create our plans of action. We look at how the external environment may change, what disruptive technologies may emerge, how customers are going to evolve, what can be the changes in policy and regulations and what kind of competition will develop. Having identified these, we look at how we can react or influence each or any of the factors. The next step is to design our strategy in a way that helps us create positive future scenarios.

So, has scenario planning delivered? Let me give you an example of what it has done for us. Even till a year back, most analysts, consultants and industry professionals said that there are too many malls and shopping centres coming up across the country. It was a standard opinion of pretty much everyone in the industry. It was based on the growth of the retail sector in the past. Considering that there were a handful of players in modern retail and a small fraction of urban population visiting shopping malls, conventional logic suggested that an overcapacity in retail real estate was round the corner.

However, within a year's time, the scenario has reversed. With a large number of big players entering the sector and modern retail reaching out to new customer segments, the industry is facing a paucity of quality retail spaces. The 600-odd malls that will be there by 2008 now seem to be less with respect to the opportunity that is unfolding. Now there is a mad rush to book spaces and retail real estate rentals have shot through the roof.

On the other hand, we always believed that the potential for modern retail was huge in India. We looked at consumer demographics, consumption patterns and what was happening at our own stores. It was evident to us that modern retail was set to grow at a rate that was far higher than how it had grown in the past. And it was foolish to assume large players wouldn't enter the sector. Since 2002, we started booking retail space much in excess of what our business plan envisaged at that point of time. We got the space at low rates and are now close to securing the entire real estate space that we plan to operate in by the year 2011. Existing and new players are now fighting for space and are inevitably paying a huge premium for it. Our growth plans, on the other hand, are not constrained by these considerations. And the benefits of a lower real estate cost structure will be reaped by none other than our customers.

Not just in real estate, but also in choosing business partners, vendors and collaborators, we were the first to get the best on board. This now gives us a significant advantage over the known and unknown face of the competition. While everyone else was debating and analysing viability in their boardrooms, we were on the road executing our plans. We knew there would be plenty of challenges that we will have to face, but we wanted to be the first to identify the opportunities that would emerge from these challenges.

V

I consider business organisations to be living, breathing entities which grow organically. And I also believe that there is a lot that organisations can learn from understanding nature. Nature is the best designer and very often we have been inspired by the way nature works. In nature, there are no fundamental tensions between conservation and change, between order and freedom, between the organised and disorganised. Complexity and simplicity coexist in nature. There is a continuous fight for survival and yet there is harmony and interdependence among all living organisms.

At face value, these aspects may seem to be mutually conflicting. But underlying them is a secular theme that cuts across everything: growth. Behind creation, evolution, adaptation and destruction, there is a constant process of growth in nature. In nature, one never sees stagnation. Just as a river always finds its way, no matter what the hindrances, an organisation too can face many roadblocks, but that need not bring it to a standstill. Physically, intellectually and financially an organisation has to evolve, adapt and move on. I call this 'flow.'

The idea of flow is extremely important for any business organisation and it is part of our organisation's core value. If one believes in the idea of flow, one always moves on rather than getting stuck and wasting time in making decisions. In most organisations, managers keep working in circles, discussing and re-discussing everything from every possible angle. And yet, of the ten decisions they make, only eight turn out to be right. Two still go wrong.

I feel that out of every ten decisions, even if eight are right, then it is very, very good. One or two decisions may be wrong in retrospect but if we hesitate because we don't have enough information or aren't sure whether something will succeed or fail, then we wouldn't be able to take advantage of all the emerging opportunities. An organisation can never have perfect information or complete consensus before leading a new initiative. There will always be some amount of conflict and a lot of uncertainty. But the moment it stops to resolve each issue and make everything certain, it moves towards stagnation. Everyone in our organisation, irrespective of what level they work in, is encouraged to take initiatives and make decisions.

However, nature also teaches us that there needs to be harmony and coexistence. *Nothing* is permanent or forever. And no one can harm another and remain unharmed himself. Anything that grows too big ultimately disintegrates. Much like in nature, business organisations too can't grow at the cost of others. I firmly believe that as an organisation, we cannot grow at the cost of our suppliers, our business partners or even the neighbourhood shops. We have to grow with the community we live in and build symbiotic relationships with everyone who is associated with us. The day we stop valuing and nurturing the relationships that we have with customers, communities, investors, business partners and vendors, we will set ourselves up for complete destruction.

I think that this twin idea of constant growth and allowing others to grow has played a crucial part in the way we have evolved as an organisation. We didn't learn this from anyone else. It didn't come from any management tome or from a session with a management guru. This lesson was evident in nature.

VI

'It's all in the genes,' is something we often say when we describe a person. And if organisations are living, breathing entities then they too have their own genes. These genes are embedded in the organisational design, its people, the human dynamics, its incentives, and the way people work within the organisation.

Since individual behaviours determine an organisation's success over time, we recently thought it was time to understand what our organisational genes are, how these have helped us reach where we are and how these will move us to a common objective. We spent a good amount of time introspecting about what makes our organisation the way it is. And we came up with the following — the Pantaloon Genes:

♦ WE LIKE BEING SIMPLE and we like simplicity in our ideas. Simple ideas help us accomplish big tasks and overcome challenges.

♦ SPEED IS THE ESSENCE OF EVERYTHING WE DO. We do plan and use numbers and data to make informed decisions. But we do not get into exaggerated planning or over-analyse things. We do not like to slow down or stop.

♦ WE LIKE TO LEARN WHILE WE EXECUTE. And to learn, we have to take risks. We may make mistakes in the process but as we keep learning from our mistakes, we never repeat them.

♦ WE LIKE THRIFT. We don't like extravagance; we don't like to flaunt fancy cars or gadgets. We want to lower costs for our customers. And we do it by continuously bringing down our own costs of operation, planning in advance and tapping cost-efficient resources.

◆ WE BELIEVE THAT CUSTOMERS ARE ALWAYS RIGHT. Customers are the reason we are in business and we learn the most from them. We actively watch them and try to understand their articulated as well as unarticulated needs. And, we like to offer them products and services even before they express their need.

◆ WE LIKE TO THINK IN TERMS OF THE MAJORITY OF PEOPLE. We do not like to be exclusivist in our approach towards customers. We also like to take into account the diversity in our country and design our customer interface according to local tastes and preferences.

◆ WE TAKE PRIDE IN OUR CORE VALUE OF INDIAN-NESS. We believe India is emerging as a different country in a different era, and it needs ideas that are uniquely Indian. We believe India will show the world how great things can be achieved differently. And we like to be the thought leaders in driving this change.

◆ WE BELIEVE IN OURSELVES. We believe in our organisation's ability to think differently and thereby achieve what many others think impossible. We like to foster a culture of innovation. We like to use both sides of the brain — the creative as well as the analytical side.

◆ WE DO NOT LIKE TO BLAME OTHERS OR EXTERNAL FACTORS. When faced with roadblocks, we like to introspect and find out whether the problem is with our organisational design, our human dynamics or our processes. Our efficiency depends on our persistent will to improve.

◆ WE LIKE TO THINK POSITIVELY IN EVERY SITUATION. We like to believe that there is always a promise hidden behind each adverse scenario. We want to take advantage of every situation, whether it looks bad or good. We believe that the future will always be brighter than today.

♦ WE LIKE BUILDING AND NURTURING RELATIONSHIPS with everyone who comes in touch with us. We like to grow with our partners. We like to grow with the society and community we operate in.

♦ WE LOVE TO REWRITE RULES, EVEN AS WE RETAIN OUR VALUES.

Business of Life

'*Give till it hurts.*'

MOTHER TERESA

I

Diwali is a time for celebration. To me it is also a time for my own appraisal. Every Diwali, I look around myself to find out whether every family member of mine is content and happy. I visualise each one's situation, put myself in their shoes and see if I would also have felt good in their place.

Over the years, one comes to realise that managing the family is no less important than managing the business. We are a fairly large family and two of my brothers and two of my cousins played a crucial role in laying the foundation for our organisation. To me, I am not just leading a company, but the family as well. And it calls for sacrifices, self discipline and practising what I preach. Among ourselves, we have a certain set of standards and nobody can cross these, not even me. Leading the family calls for a very different kind of leadership which is far more empathetic and soft. And it is something I am proud to have done quite well.

One of the most necessary steps we took was to completely separate ownership, governance and execution. For ownership, we formed trusts that collectively own the shares we have in the company. No two people are equal and everyone has their own strengths, weaknesses, abilities and disabilities. We recognise these and have taken upon different roles that suit our abilities and complement our strengths.

Within the organisation, we family members mostly concentrate on building and nurturing relationships with business partners and on providing an overall guidance to the business. When it comes to taking business decisions they are equal to the other professionals in the company. We all have our differences and disagreements.

But everyone speaks out openly about these and it is very reassuring for me. It shows the conviction everyone has and their determination to stand by it. We may have different views, different approaches towards business but our overall feelings are in the best interests of the company. We call this 'collective individualism' — multiple beliefs but a single goal. There is no backstabbing, no animosity, no jealousy in our joint family and that to me is a big achievement.

My cousin Rakesh, my uncle Gopalji and myself represent the family on the board of Pantaloon Retail. Our board also has six independent directors. All our independent directors come from very diverse backgrounds and form a strong framework for governance. The board reviews the performance of the company. And we have a team of professionals who lead the day-to-day executive functions within the organisation and the executive powers lie in their hands.

My biggest critics are inside my house. My daughters, Ashni and Avni are my biggest inspirations as well as my staunchest critics. Whenever they are shopping at our stores along with their mother — and that happens quite often with three women in the family — I expect a few calls on what is good, bad and ugly inside the stores.

Ashni and Avni along with their cousins, Vivek and Nishita, provide me with an immediate connect with the new generation. Youth brings with it a lot of irreverence and an eagerness to challenge every belief. Between the four of them, they constantly provoke new thoughts in me, challenge my beliefs and point out my mistakes. And that to me is very reassuring. I know that it is only their judgement that isn't based on any fear, prejudice or vested interest.

I tend to believe that the reason we have been relatively happy as a family is because we have been able to retain the middle class ethos that we grew up with. Respect, humility, and simplicity — these are some of the values that still bind us together. Our company's financial strength may have grown, but I don't think that has brought any difference in the way we are and behave. I leave my house by nine in the morning and when I am in Mumbai, I am always back home before nine in the evening. Socialising and partying is not my cup of tea. And though I may not be able to go for all my daughter's school functions, my family knows that I will be available when they need me. It's the same with my friends and relatives who have known me for a long time.

HIRU THAKURDAS*

Kishoreji has become so big today from the business point of view. But I have never known that from him. I have come to know it from magazines, newspapers and outsiders. The confidence and passion with which he speaks about his ideas was pretty much the same even two decades back. He may hide his emotions well, but he still trusts people blindly. He values every relationship as much as he did ten years back. His lifestyle, his desires have remained pretty much the same. He still wears the same set of trousers for years. And when it comes to carrying money in his pocket, he still hardly has any. Many a times, I bail him out for his petrol bill or lunch bill. The world

*Hiru Thakurdas has been a close friend and associate of Kishore.

around Kishoreji may have changed, but he is still the same person I had come to know twenty-five years back.

I have now slowly come to realise that recognition and fame come with their own set of advantages and disadvantages. There are times when I feel privileged. I get invited by the so-called 'high and mighty' for parties and functions. Once in a while, I am invited to meet the head of a foreign country. At other times I get to represent the industry or even the country at international forums and that definitely is a proud moment. Minor irritants — not entirely dissimilar to unsolicited tele-marketing calls — crop up, like when the Marketing Director of a luxury car brand repeatedly invited me for a luncheon meeting so that he could hard-sell the latest model to me.

People now recognise me at the most unusual of locations, from airport foyers to hotel washrooms. Over time one learns to get comfortable with it, often at one's own peril. And sometimes, when people do not recognise me at public places, unconsciously I feel something is different, something seems to be missing.

However, the biggest casualty is often the personal relationships with friends and acquaintances. People I have known for decades have begun to think that I am too busy and avoid calling me. Close friends think twice before dropping in at my office unannounced, lest they disturb me. Such presumptions can be extremely disturbing at times.

II

I believe that we all come to this world to kill time. Therefore, we pick up some activity that we like doing and call it our profession. I call this the Time Pass theory.

I am an entrepreneur. I work to build a business, an organisation. But what I am essentially doing is trying to spend the time I have in this lifetime. Every morning, when I am busy getting ready to leave for work or some meeting, I am doing it not because I have to do it. I am doing it because I will not have much else to do through the day.

We all get busy in our professions so that we can enjoy the time we spend at work and perform something that we think is productive. Some people choose teaching as a profession, some people choose to be sailors and some choose to be professional writers. And through this work-life of ours, we tend to create our own world. We make our own definitions of success and failure, of victories and defeats. And we use these not only to judge our own selves, but also to judge others, without ever realising that what we all are doing is basically digging holes and filling them up. Yet I have seen so many people take their life too seriously, not realising that what they are essentially doing in this world is time pass.

Different people have different ways of measuring success. Some people measure success by the car they drive, their job title, the grades they received in school, the college they graduated from or the awards and recognition society has showered over them. We all live in our own shells — have our exclusive admirers and critics. We love to inspect ourselves in the mirror, either to reprimand or pat ourselves on the back. And when someone becomes known to the public, he or she lives by the mirror of the newspapers or television channels. Many of them, I have found, decide their success by the number of times they have appeared on television or the number of times their name or photo appears in the newspapers. And whether it was glossy paper, pink paper or plain white newsprint, too starts to count!

Soon after our company had won some awards, I had a stimulating conversation with my daughter. She asked me what success means to me. Is it measurable, or is it relative and subjective?

Success to me is about attaining a certain sensibility that one finds within oneself. This sensibility is something I cannot measure or define. It is about a particular moment, an instance, an expression, an experience that is realised. Each human being is entitled to set his or her own goals, parameters and beliefs that shape their route and directs them to their success story. To me every individual is inherently special and successful in some way or the other.

For me, when I consider all that I have been able to achieve I am glad to say that I have not achieved it by going against the flow of nature. I have never complicated or got hung up about unnecessary things. I have always looked at the end goal and pursued it with all my passion. But when faced with tough challenges, I have chosen to take the lesser travelled road, instead of being confrontational and uncompromising.

Even in the competitive arena of business, I have let the flow take me over and lead me to the simple satisfaction of doing a job well. I could never have found happiness by stepping on someone else's toes. To me 'flow' implies immersing oneself fully into what one does. It is characterised by a feeling of energised focus, genuine involvement, and success in the *process* of the activity.

People outside our organisation perceive us quite differently from how they did even a few years back. The media attention and the awards we have received are popular expressions of how the world views us now. We have been fortunate to receive several such accolades and I am thankful for all of them. But these can only provide momentary sensations of happiness or success. Even a big win against the competition or getting a new partner for our business, are all transient accomplishments. I choose to interpret them in another way. All the attention, awards and recognition actually bring along a strong sense of responsibility of meeting millions of expectations.

For me, that can be achieved only when I am truly tuned into my environment and am willing to go with its flow. This flow allows me to understand continuity, customer responses, aspirations and growth. And the fulfilment I experience when I see happy shoppers outside our stores, when I see more customers carrying our shopping bags or when I see the simple smiles of pleasure on the faces of our customers, is far greater than any award I have got till date.

III

Everyone is entitled to their own definition of success. And so it is with failure. It is tough to define failure and even tougher to measure it. Just as there are social benchmarks for success, are there such benchmarks for failure as well? Is failure the opposite of success? And can merely making a mistake be equated with failure?

I have discovered that people who do not blame others for slip-ups or setbacks are the ones who are the happiest. These people do not use other's definitions for success or failure either. They use their own. I believe that missing a target, changing paths or trying something new cannot and should not be treated as failures. True failure happens only when individuals stop trying to achieve their personal best.

In the mid-Nineties when we tried selling our branded trousers to a large retail chain, they were rejected. After having built a nation-wide chain of franchisee stores, we had to close it down. Even in the recent past, some of our retail concepts didn't turn out the way we wanted. But we were never discouraged by any of these. All these experiences gave us some amount of learning and we used it to improve our strategies and build better businesses.

Similarly, my attempt at making movies wasn't successful at all. And it was a humbling experience. But I would not be what I am, if I had not made these movies.

Failures like these, I believe, have been steady steps towards success for our organisation. A failure is not final by itself. It is, instead, an opportunity to learn, improve and move on. In fact I don't think setbacks, disappointments, rejections, or unsuccessful attempts can be even called failures. A sudden setback can be seen as a brick wall. It can also be seen as a stepping stone.

Most people, however, are unable to acknowledge their oversights or mistakes. I feel it is crucial for an individual to be prepared to laugh at himself. Recognising that one has made a mistake — even in a small way — and learning from it, is the first step towards success. Absolute failure actually happens when one stops trying to do new things; it's about total lack of conviction in one's own ideas and aspirations; and it's about giving up. And I don't think I will ever reach the state of absolute failure, because I am not a person who gives up, at least not without waging a war.

IV

War holds a negative connotation and most of us associate it with destruction and devastation. But war is a reality which is not limited to the defence forces; *everyone* has to fight wars — big or small, alone or with friends, forced or unforced. It is part of the cycle of creation, preservation and destruction. War is also about the art of strategy; about the state of mental preparedness. And at any point of life, one has to be prepared to fight a war.

I think the first principle in war is to know what to fight and when to fight. It is important to choose one's battles. One must be aware, not only of the ultimate goal, but also of one's strengths and weaknesses. Only fools get into every battle. One should know which battles one has to win and which battles one can afford to lie low in. For smart fighters, the objective is not to win every battle, but to win the war.

I also believe that to fight a successful war, one needs to free oneself from attachment and prejudice. One cannot get passionate and subjective about anything during the war. The moment one gets attached to something, he creates a weakness for the enemy to attack. To detach oneself and fight is the only way to do justice to the war and emerge victorious.

However, the best wars are those that are won without fighting or what I call 'mind games.' These are obviously the toughest wars to fight, where one has to defeat the enemy strategically and psychologically. One has to know, or rather predict, each possible move of the enemy way before he makes it. It could also mean creating an illusionary war. It could mean making the enemy commit a tactical mistake. It could also mean that one creates a situation where the verdict is evident even before the end of the war!

But war is only a euphemism, not limited to the competition. When it comes to competition, I feel it is a healthy way of ensuring the development and growth of societies. Individuals and organisations should always be inspired and enthusiastic about evolving and climbing further and further up the ladder of development. The most important aspect of this evolution is to take one's society along; and create a symbiotic energy that will be beneficial for all those who come in contact with the developing individual or organisation. That is what my aim of 'war' finally is.

V

In the early chapters of the book I had discussed how it is not easy to find mentors or role models to pursue one's dreams. I did not have any real role models or mentors but it was from reading books, magazines and newspapers that I formed my own 'mental' role models, learnt about business and shaped my outlook towards life. Most of the ideas expressed in this book are in many ways influenced by what I have read in all these years. This book will be incomplete if I did not also talk about some of the books that have influenced me.

A book I would like to recommend to everyone is Stephen Covey's *The 7 Habits of Highly Effective People*. It provides a step-by-step framework for living and working, based on some fundamental principles or natural laws. I read this book when I was quite young and it influenced me a lot. I have actually found these habits to be existent in every successful person I have met. Another equally motivating book is Anthony Robbins' *Awaken the Giant Within*. It explores how every human being can live up to their true potential. Paulo Coelho's *The Alchemist* and Richard Bach's *Jonathan Livingstone Seagull* have inspired many of us within the organisation and helped us achieve what others thought impossible.

Futurist writer Alvin Toffler in his trilogy, *Future Shock*, *The Third Wave* and *Powershift* examines the reaction to changes in society brought about by technology and culture. In one of his most fascinating insights, he states, 'The illiterate of the twenty-first century will not be those who cannot read and write, but those who cannot learn, unlearn, and relearn.' And then there is Tom Peters who challenges the status quo, sees chaos as a foundation for creativity and stresses on the importance of design thinking — ideas integral to our organisation. Peters' books, *A Passion for Excellence* and *Re-Imagine* are both provocative and inspiring. The thought process with which we are today building our organisation is in fact quite similar to that of Tom Peters.

On retail, a book that has had the maximum impact on the way we do business is of course Sam Walton's *Made in America*. However, there are very few books on retail I haven't read. Among my favourites is Howard Schultz's *Pour Your Heart Into It: How Starbucks Built a Company One Cup at a Time*. Schultz proved that it is simplicity and passion coupled with a spirit of innovation that lies at the root of creating a great consumer experience. There are other equally fascinating books written on retailers like Bernie Marcus and Arthur Blank's *How a Couple of Regular Guys Grew The Home Depot from Nothing to $30 billion*; Ingvar Kamprad's *Leading By Design: The IKEA Story*; and Marvin Traub's *Like No Other Store: The Bloomingdale's Legend and Revolution in American Marketing*.

I have also read my fair share of autobiographies written by foreign and Indian entrepreneurs. But no book strikes me more than Verghese Kurien's autobiography, *I Too Had a Dream*. Kurien's story is of a genuine Indian folk hero. He proves that if one has the conviction and ability to unleash the power of ordinary Indians, one can turn any dream into reality. In terms of its sheer relevance in the current Indian context, the book easily stands out in comparison with what I have read on Indian business. Throughout the book,

Kurien reiterates that the biggest asset of India is its people and states, 'We have glorious examples in our country of what our people can achieve — and have achieved — by working together.'

Kurien isn't shy of pointing out the disturbing truth, 'The tragedy of India is that we have no respect for Indians, for Indian efforts and for Indian successes.' It is sad that all the issues that Kurien faced — the opportunistic attitude of multinationals, lack of public leadership, bureaucratic bottlenecks — continue to be the biggest challenges India faces even today. However, what this book proves is that even after fifty years since the Kaira Cooperative Union was formed, the basic tenets of success pretty much remain the same: trust in people, belief in oneself and pride in one's country.

But if you think that I have always ended up reading the supposedly 'boring business books,' you are wrong. As a kid, we didn't have Cartoon Network and Nickelodeon. Sundays were spent reading *Tintin, Asterix, Archie* and *Richie Rich*. I was also a big fan of popular fiction writers like Robert Ludlum whose stories always revolved around one man or a small group of individuals who successfully fought powerful adversaries. There are other writers like Irving Wallace who wrote, 'To be oneself, and unafraid whether right or wrong, is more admirable than the easy cowardice of surrender to conformity.' Equally interesting were the innumerable thrillers of James Hadley Chase.

However, to understand the Indian context one has to read books written in Indian languages. Though I have read such books only in Hindi, I am sure that all Indian languages have books that provide rich insights about how we live and work, and naturally provide the truest picture of our country. Munshi Premchand's simplicity and honest rendition of the problems and dilemmas of the urban middle class, for instance, transcends both time and geography.

Most of the successful Hindi authors went through their own struggles in life which are captured in their books. Harivansh Rai Bachchan's poems are a reflection of his own life, the poverty, the tragedies, the achievements and the bouts of bliss. The same holds true for Kamleshwar whose work depicts the trials and tribulations of a fast-changing urban society. Harishanker Parsai deals with everyday issues like corruption and exploitation and treats them with a unique sense of sarcasm and humour. These Hindi authors have left a lasting impression on my understanding of Indian society and human behaviour.

Who Says Elephants Can't Dance?

'Survival and success depend on speed and imagination.'

N.R. NARAYANA MURTHY

I

Every organisation needs a Brahma, a Vishnu, and a Shiva — a creator, a preserver, and a destroyer. For an organisation to grow and keep pace with the changing reality, it needs these tensions simultaneously. What happens with many organisations is that after they attain a certain size, the preservers take over and stagnation sets in. I consider myself to be a creator and destroyer first. I never really had much of the 'preserver' instinct in me.

To begin with, every three years we have destroyed our existing organisational design. Let me illustrate how we created new things out of this destruction. We started off as a garment manufacturer and subsequently launched a few brands. The business at that time was focussed on the fashion segment and for a brief period we called ourselves Pantaloon Fashion House. The next step was to establish our own retail chain for our fashion products and slowly thereafter we built multiple retail businesses.

Reaching out directly to consumers required a thorough understanding of different customer segments. For us, gathering this knowledge was the prime focus. It would prove to be the biggest weapon at our disposal in an environment where everything else was temporary and transient. Our quest for knowledge had to be methodical and systematic. So we formed the Pantaloon Knowledge Group and created a knowledge office within the company to act as the key driver and assimilator of information. A vast repository of insights and understanding on retail and Indian consumers helped us understand both the articulated as well as unarticulated needs of customers, set new trends and exceed the expectations of our stakeholders.

In 2006, we took the next big leap. With almost a decade of retailing, we realised that the time was right for us to leverage the knowledge and create a company based on ideas and innovation. Our earlier organisational design was meant for running a sustainable retail business. But the emerging opportunities allowed us to look at the entire consumption space. Future Group was the outcome of the new thinking that has come into the organisation. We have destroyed the earlier structure to create a new design that can serve as a platform for multiple ideas and businesses in the consumption space.

That's the destroyer in me. The creator can be seen in the unique designing of the organisation. The organisation is now based on scenario planning, design thinking, innovation and ideas, and new areas of research like memetics. Neither do we look at the past, nor do we base our decisions on what has already happened. We look at the future and create a lot of scenarios for the future: how the organisation can look like three years down line, what are the challenges that can come up, etc. Then we develop an organisational strategy and try to create favourable business scenarios for the future. The intention is to fix a problem even before it appears and leverage an opportunity before anyone else has noticed it.

As a leader of the organisation, my role is to provide a holistic picture and a strategic direction to the group. I have my own weaknesses. I had led the day-to-day operations of the business for a fairly long time during the initial phase of our business. In the Eighties and Nineties, I was learning while executing. At this stage however, I think my abilities are far better utilised in a strategic role, rather than in an execution role.

We now have a phenomenal team of professionals that takes care of the day-to-day operations of our business. I leave it to this team to make the decisions at the ground level and execute them. A symphony conductor is usually a great director, but not necessarily a world-class performer himself. I think I have been able to build a team that believes in my vision and have successfully passed on the values and ethos that have helped us reach this stage.

I am also very impulsive by nature. And I cannot really say 'no' comfortably: I trust people a lot and these can be weaknesses as well as strengths. But my core strengths lie in my ability to envision the future, my ability to understand human dynamics, and my ability to act fast. The decisions I take are mostly strategic in nature. Apart from that most of my time is spent on meeting people and building valuable relationships.

I am also not a perfectionist. I don't believe there is some 'perfect world' and I find it is more fruitful to search for excellence rather than perfection. Problems begin when we look for perfection everywhere. It's a futile search. Imperfection can be something to enjoy and be content with. We should take pleasure in who we are and do what makes us happy.

SANJAY JOG*

When I joined the company, one of my biggest concerns was that there were more than forty people who were directly reporting to the Managing Director. The number has only doubled since then. This completely runs against the concept of an ideal organisational design. The first impression one gets is that here is a man who wants to run a one-man show.

It took some time for me to realise that for Kishoreji there is a difference between direct access and direct reports.

---

*Sanjay Jog is the Head of Human Resources at Pantaloon Retail.

He wants to be in the thick of things and be in a position where anyone and everyone can walk into his office and discuss something. But he is not a person who gets into the nitty-gritty of things. He is willing to provide the broad objectives but not the road map. He never peeps into our daily work.

As the leader he plays the role of a coach and a sounding board for self-managing teams. His objective is to institutionalise ideation and execution within teams. And wherever required he is eager to bring in cross-functional system support or outside help. Most leaders look for things that went wrong and try to fix them. Kishoreji looks for things that went right and tries to build on them. He doesn't fear people making mistakes. He fears the absence of creative, constructive and entrepreneurial energy in people and in teams.

I believe that leadership is not about delegation. Leadership is about abdication, and there is a significant difference there. With delegation one still tries to retain the overall supervisory control of the job. But that isn't good enough. It creates an army of preservers whose only aim is to preserve the status quo and follow pre-defined rules set by the leader. To drive innovation and entrepreneurship, a leader needs to abdicate most decision-making and executive roles to his team. Only then can a leader move on to a higher level and achieve something bigger and better for the organisation. This belief of allowing team members to take decisions has now cascaded to every level in our organisation. And that is one of the very important reasons why we have been able to get into so many businesses and managed to grow each one of them at a fast pace.

Many of our new businesses now function independently of Pantaloon Retail. They are managed by people who have years of experience in some of the best companies in India and abroad. One of them is Sameer Sain, who relocated from London to Mumbai to become a partner in our financial arm, Future Capital.

Yet, as partners we are as different as chalk and cheese. He comes from a very structured background, has been to one of the best B-schools and is far more cautious when it comes to decision-making. He has spent most of his life abroad, likes to lead a good lifestyle and is a charmer by nature. There are a whole lot of issues that we have agreed to disagree on. But there are two things common between us. We both love old Hindi film music and are equally passionate about building the financial business. Sameer believes, and rightly so, that the capital business needs a whole new set of capabilities, knowledge and a culture that is very different from our retail business. His aspiration to build the best financial services company in India, matches our ambition to serve everything to the every Indian customer in the best possible manner. And that is good enough reason for me to leave the entire management of the business to him.

SAMEER SAIN*

During my eleven year tenure at Goldman Sachs, and especially as a Managing Director within its Wealth Management business, I had the opportunity to closely

---

*Sameer Sain is the Managing Director of Future Capital Holdings. Prior to taking over this role, in January 2006, he served as a Managing Director in Goldman Sachs (Europe).

interact with some of the smartest and most successful entrepreneurs. While many of them have several common characteristics such as drive, determination and a certain irrational risk-taking ability, they also have several differences. They come in all shapes and sizes and range from visionaries to operators, aggressive to passive, kind-hearted to ruthless, imperialists to wealth creators, and the egotistical to the humble. Yet, there are few who inspire entrepreneurship; fewer who teach you how to dream; and hardly any who will actually embrace your potential, mentor you unselfishly and cherish your success. Kishore is a man of contradictions and his management style reflects his personality. He loves using oxymorons and he is best described by using them. He is a shy aggressor, a visionary operator, and a non-confrontational warrior. It is therefore understandable why at first his management style is very confusing. He has a timid handshake and will not look you in the eye, but he will make extremely bold statements and aggressive decisions. He can take you to one hundred thousand feet with his vision and perspective, yet get very focussed on a tiny detail at the ground level. He only talks of growth and building something great, yet will be sharply focussed on the P&L (profit and loss) and hates losing or wasting a single rupee. He will be consistently critical and shoot down almost everything you say, yet you will find a lot of your thoughts being implemented. When needed, he will always emerge as your most ardent supporter.

To someone who comes from a more structured and consistent background, Kishore is a difficult man to understand. Yet all those who know him for a long time will agree that he has made a huge difference to them, both personally and professionally. He teaches you to dream the impossible and then believe that you can achieve it. When you do, you get no credit or acknowledgement, but a reminder that he told you so. His philosophies such as 'Go with the Flow' or his theory of 'Time Pass' sound strange and un-commercial. It is easy to poke holes at them, but he will live by these theories, and time and again they have proved to be precise and commercial. For an awkwardly shy and private man, his understanding of people and their psychology is quite scary. He is able to read people within seconds and adjusts his interaction accordingly, not in a manipulative way, but in a manner where he is able to go up or down to their level without compromising his character.

Kishore has his share of weaknesses as well which are reflected in his management style. He believes that most people are not able to understand him well and therefore do not recognise his real potential and success. This accentuates the natural rebel within him and therefore he is attracted to non-conformists in general, sometimes at his peril. As a result, people around him know that if they want to get his attention, they have to 'Rewrite the Rules.' He has been persecuted by the establishment while he was trying to emerge as an entrepreneur and therefore generally abhors the establishment. So, people from the establishment who join him rarely stand a chance, irrespective of their potential. Finally, even though he thrives on feedback and constructive criticism, he makes it very difficult for people to be critical of him. Most of the time he will not listen and sometimes he will simply dismiss or outright reject their views; however, he does actually take things on board. Either way, it is a hellish experience to criticise or disagree with Kishore Biyani and, with the exception of his two daughters, most rarely do.

At the end of the day, one has to only look at the outcome. Kishore has managed to build a large organisation that has a strong culture of creativity. He has recruited talented people at all levels, including the more senior positions and somehow made them feel loyal to him and his ideas. He may have a contradictory management style, but it is these contradictions that attract all sorts of people. To quote Kishore's favourite saying, 'Strength always lies in differences.'

II

When an organisation is small, it can take decisions based on instinct and gut. But as it grows larger, decision-making has to become scientific and accurate. We are at a similar juncture wherein we need to make quicker and more informed decisions, so that we are able to scale up faster and better. While we have grown at a steady pace, at times growth may have come at the cost of setting up efficient systems and processes at the operational level. Our tolerance of operational quality standards may also have been lower than usual.

An area of concern for most outsiders has been our back-end. Our initial focus had been on getting the front-end or the customer interface right. We didn't invest heavily in our back-end during the initial phase and that was intentional. We didn't want to get into a situation where our back-end would become incompatible with the kind of front-end we built. We have now got our customer interface right and it is time for us to improve efficiency and build a robust back-end for our entire business. And in this, I see technology playing a major role.

In the last couple of years, we have experimented with a lot of different technologies. In 2005, we implemented an RFID pilot-project at our warehouses. We were the first retailer in India to use this technology. RFID is a chip-based technology that can be attached to each and every product that is sold at a retail outlet. This then helps a retailer to keep track of every product as it moves from the supplier to the warehouse to the store, and finally to the customer's shopping basket. For the customer, it means faster and easier billing. The retailer on the other hand not only has real-time information of each and every product that is being sold, but also where and how it is moving across the supply chain. I believe that RFID has the potential to completely transform the entire retailing industry. However, the technology itself is yet to mature and is currently too expensive to implement across any retail chain.

In 2006, we rolled out SAP, an enterprise resource planning tool that allows us to control and manage our inventory in a far more efficient way. While we are yet to utilise the full potential of both RFID technology and SAP, our experience at implementing these has provided valuable insights and understanding on how we can use IT to deliver more value and convenience to customers.

Therefore, we are now in a far better a position to bring in more technology-driven processes and systems and are partnering with some of the best technology companies in the world. Having a low technology base, as of now, has its own set of advantages — we do not have any of the legacy systems that other global retailers have. We can start afresh and build an entirely new set of technological back-end that wouldn't get obsolete in the near future. New technology can also bring a transformational change in terms of business efficiencies, market forecasting and customer conveniences.

We are looking at various technology options that will improve all-round visibility of performance and manage a seamless flow of information across the organisation. We want to tighten our control mechanisms, make businesses more efficient and build robust platforms to make our business grow. Technology will also help us deliver more value to customers through better forecasting, inventory management and collaborative planning.

Predictive analytics and artificial intelligence are exciting areas and I would love to have the power to predict the future with these tools. We want to understand more about our customers and analyse a lot of behaviour patterns. Once we consolidate all our consumer data at the group level, we will try to introduce predictive analytics and intelligence to help us foresee trends more precisely.

One of our first initiatives in this area is going to be the launch of a retail back-end technology services company, Future Knowledge Services. Leading this initiative is Ushir Bhatt, who has led technology initiatives at some of the largest retail chains in Europe. This subsidiary will help us build a back-end for our design services and business process outsourcing. It will take care of all repetitive tasks in accounting, finance, payroll management, customer relationship management and other areas across group companies.

However, I look at information technology as a tool, which coupled with human interpretation skills, can help arrive at the best decisions quickly. Technology is only as good as the people using it. IT can only help us get information but interpreting information into tacit and explicit knowledge that will benefit the business can only be done by human beings. The belief that technology alone can help one do good business is fundamentally faulty. The success of our business will continue to depend on our human potential. But technology can be the most critical enabler.

USHIR BHATT*

The Future Group is at the point of inflection. However, we have realised that the existing technology and processes will not be able to cope with the huge growth that is expected. This is a big challenge and an even bigger opportunity.
Kishore has an uncanny ability to spot customer trends and turn them into profitable opportunities. In his early days he claimed that technology would play little role in retail. Today he is a convert because he recognises that the scale of operations and breadth of offerings being built by the group demands nothing less than a complete overhaul of systems and processes. The ability to create something, destroy it and create something new, at the

---

*Ushir Bhatt is CEO, Future Knowledge Services and joined the group in January 2007. In his earlier role, he was instrumental in setting up the Tesco Hindustan Service Centre in Bangalore.

right time for the new scenario, is one of Kishore's biggest strengths.

The opportunity to destroy the 'as is' scenario allows us to leapfrog the processes of existing retailers because we have no legacy to deal with. Concepts like Social Retailing™ — technology that explores how to engage the tech-savvy young customers in a unique way, even while expanding retail sales and reach — viral networking, RFID and the mobile revolution, all underpinned by a solid transaction processing capability, will be at the heart of creating newer and better customer experiences. Using innovation and knowledge to implement transformational ways of working will sustain the organisation for the long-term. The new mantra should be about customer, location and process underpinned by technology.

Weaved into all of this is the Indian environment with all its diversity and complexity. My own past experience across a number of industries and countries over the last thirty years makes me believe that applying simplicity to the organised chaos that is India is the answer to a lot of problems. The journey, of course, has just begun and I think it is going to be fun.

Working with Kishore is much like drinking Guinness, in other words, it's an acquired taste. So the challenge of explaining the 'what and the why of technology' is going to be fun. At the same time, given his excitable style and short span of attention, it's also going to be very frustrating. However I suspect he's a closet technology guy, so I'm looking forward to it.

III

We have set for ourselves a fairly ambitious target for the year 2011. By that time we plan to operate 30 million square feet of retail space. These will be spread in over hundred cities across the country and it should translate into a turnover of Rs 30,000 crore. Reaching such an ambitious target is definitely not going to be easy and there are plenty of challenges ahead. In terms of the sheer size of our operations, it means that we will have to grow ten times bigger during a five-year period. Basic calculations show that in order to reach this size we should be able to service over three crore customers every week and process over thirty crore bills every year. It will require more people, real estate, resources and appropriate technology to manage growth.

Tools like scenario planning have helped us build a good foundation for enabling growth. In terms of space, we have secured almost the entire real estate properties we will require till the year 2011. And with respect to people, I do not think in a nation of a billion people there can be a shortage of personnel. To continuously bring in talented manpower into our businesses, we are collaborating with around a dozen educational institutions to train and recruit people for our organisation. Our attrition levels being far lower than the industry average, we have been able to build a solid foundation for growth and continuity.

At the macro-economic level, we have looked at how our business would perform under various scenarios. That includes how we can scrape through a deep recession in the economy. A major economic recession in the next five years is almost an impossibility. Yet, we have de-risked ourselves fairly well for that eventuality as well. We are present in multiple categories of retailing and in both the value and the lifestyle segments. Even if there is a shift towards lesser-value products, due to an economic downturn, we will be able to attract a lot of customers through our value business.

Also, our retailing business does not have a very high capital-intensive model and our interest cost has come down significantly. One of the highest fixed costs that we pay is the rentals for the real estate that we occupy. However, the way we have structured our agreements allow us to vacate properties early, even in worst-case scenarios. We may not be fully immune to an economic depression, but we are sufficiently protected, much more than many other businesses. Our margins are low, and this can impact us, but in business one can minimise risk only to a certain extent.

Going forward, each of our new businesses — asset management, consumer finance, insurance, retail media and real estate management — can bring in substantially higher profit margins than our retail business. Retail will continue to be the nucleus of the group and it will also help us attract more customers and thereby grow these businesses. This in turn will help us boost our bottom-line.

However, the major challenge for us is actually to retain our soul, our values and our approach towards business. Many have called it an irreverent attitude, a contrarian view, and even a maverick behaviour. But the fact is that our way of working, our way of interpreting the market has worked extraordinarily well for us.

ANANTH RAMAN*

Much like any other business, Pantaloon Retail will go through massive short-term disruptions. There will be bad

---

*Ananth Raman is a UPS Foundation Professor of Business Logistics at the Harvard Business School. He has co-authored a case study on Big Bazaar.

quarters or even a bad financial year. No company can avoid that and it isn't unusual or fatal for the company. However, the risk that I see is that because of these short-term disruptions, the management may end up questioning the basic business model that has brought it the success in the first place. Because of a bad quarter or a bad year, the management may lose faith in its own understanding of the business. That I see as the major risk. Many companies have gone through this kind of a situation.

I remember attending a presentation being made by a senior executive of a large retailer, during the dotcom era. This successful retailer was planning to launch a portal that would cater to the B2B segment. I was surprised by the whole thing; nothing could be more disastrous than a successful retailer planning a B2B foray, instead of focussing on retail consumers. An investor who was also present there quipped in saying that these days the words 'dotcom' and 'B2B' earn a higher valuation.

We are also getting into different businesses in the consumption space, where the challenges may be quite different from what we have encountered till now. While some of our businesses are maturing, some are still at a very early stage. Yet, there is no reason to think that the values we have cherished all these years need to be changed. It may be easy to implement a tried and tested foreign solution for a new business, but it will most probably not work in India. Belief in self and belief in the Indian way of doing things is our fundamental principle.

We may have grown larger and more powerful, but we still need to conduct ourselves with the same humility and respect in our relationships with our supply partners. In fact, we have grown *because* of the relationships we have built with our business partners, communities and customers and we have to continue to nurture them. Along with this, simplicity and thrift need to be retained so that we can pass on every benefit to our customers.

Rewriting rules may have become a habit for most of us. Retaining our values will be equally important as we move forward.

Every month a large number of new people join our team and the challenge for us is to ensure that the organisational DNA remains intact. Even though our organisational size may increase manifold, we need to continue working in a seamless and agile manner. We have to float like a butterfly and sting like a bee, no matter what size or shape we acquire.

Our communication too has to match our speed of growth so that everybody within the organisation is aligned with it. One of my major lessons is that the need for communication is far, far higher than what is usually anticipated. Our communication style and processes are changing as a consequence. We are in the process of disseminating and sharing information and knowledge much more than earlier. It is a democratic and transparent process with lots of people coming together and developing multiple scenarios. The process would also include the trickling down of information and provoking every colleague to think differently, think creatively.

A personal initiative that I started more than six months ago has turned into a powerful tool to align everyone in the organisation with the common goals. Every Monday morning I pen down the dominant thoughts that have crossed my mind the preceding week. Along with it I also write down what were the major initiatives taken in the previous week and what we are planning to do in the days ahead. This goes out to every colleague through email and is called Monday Musings. This simple initiative has generated some of the most fascinating ideas and suggestions and provoked a lot of debate and discussion within our organisation.

IREENA VITTAL*

A lot of companies in India and China are going through a hyper-growth phase and many of them might suddenly fail. Part of it has to do with the strategy that they adopt. But beyond that the real challenge steps in when an organisation tries to create the capacity and capability to accelerate. More often than not, the biggest impediment to growth is organisational capacity. The other significant challenge is of creating a leadership of change during this phase of growth.

I think Kishore is cognisant of these new challenges. He is extremely confident about himself and his ideas. And somebody as innovative as Kishore will be obsessed with strategy. He gets his joy from it and it goes back to the kind of person he is. But he isn't a university academician. He needs to translate his overall vision into actionable steps.

Kishore can no longer be driven by what he wants. He has to driven by what the business needs. The question for him is whether this is the right time for him to completely abdicate himself from execution. Execution

---

*Ireena Vittal is a Partner at the consultancy firm, McKinsey & Co. She heads the firm's retail practice in India.

too involves strategy and my wish is that Kishore starts taking joy from seeing his strategy in execution. If he puts as much focus on execution as he puts on strategy and sees the beauty of execution, he will get the joy. For Kishore, the critical point should be, what is the pace, what is the time to step back, and what is the time to step up.

I fully agree that our biggest challenge would now be about managing change, both at the organisational level as well as in the external environment. The organisational capability that was required to deliver half a billion dollar turnover is significantly lower than what it will take to reach a six billion dollar figure in five years. The vision and the strategy we have put in place are primed to deliver on the targets we have set for ourselves. However, it requires a broader leadership bandwidth to manage change brought about by external factors.

Over the last couple of years, we have been successful in attracting talented professionals to our organisation. Our senior management team today is made up of people who have grown within the organisation. But they are also being joined by professionals who have worked as chief executives and business heads of large Indian and multinational companies. A fair number of them have also been independent entrepreneurs at some point or the other. It is definitely easier today to attract senior people across industries. So, collectively, they provide direction to our different businesses.

However, all our businesses are now at different stages of growth and maturity. While some of our retail businesses like Big Bazaar, Pantaloons and Central have attained some level of maturity, there are lot of new businesses that need time, resources and people to mature. Compared to our older businesses, the new businesses require different control mechanisms, different designs, different competencies and different knowledge bases.

We are therefore bringing in a new organisational design that will address these needs. The new design will bring in more accountability in each of our businesses and help the organisation operate in a far more seamless manner.

For me, the journey has begun once again in building each of these businesses and giving shape to our dreams and aspirations. Today, I have a personal mission. I know that I have come into existence to live, to learn and to leave behind a legacy — a legacy of discovering the Indian way of building an organisation, and of leveraging the opportunities that each new era brings in. And in the process I hope, that as an organisation, we will be able to play a key role in shaping the India of tomorrow.

It's a truly a new era that is emerging. The changes and opportunities that are coming forth allow us to rewrite the rules once again. Only that the pace of change is going to be much faster than what has ever been seen before and the old rules can no longer be applicable. In the new economy, business will acquire a new dimension and the approach towards it will have to be totally different. We call this the Creative Economy.

IV

This new era that is unfolding amidst us is characterised by ideas, imagination and innovation. It took thousands of years for human society to progress from an agricultural economy to an industrial economy. People who owned land were the wealthiest and most powerful in the agricultural economy. With the advent of the steam engine, railroads, large factories and assembly line manufacturing, industrial economy set in and with it the form of wealth also changed. The last century marked the transition from the industrial economy to the 'knowledge economy.' The most influential and powerful individuals and organisations derived their strength from knowledge and information. However, within a few decades of the knowledge economy, we are again witnessing a major shift.

Knowledge as we know it is being commoditised. What was once central to organisations — systems, processes and much of the left-brain, digitised analytical work associated with knowledge — is being outsourced. The most successful organisations in this new era are the ones that harness ideas, creativity and innovation to generate top-line growth.

The overarching feature of the twenty-first century society is integration. The world is increasingly being interwoven. Whether it is an individual, a company or a country: the threats and opportunities come from sources they may not even be aware of. With changing demographic profiles, seamless flow of ideas and information across the world and the increasing influence of the media, societies are evolving and changing rapidly. Change is no longer incremental, it is transformational.

Earlier, technology changed our way of life once in a few decades. The introduction of radio, television, air travel and satellite communication added to the development of society. Today, technology changes everything fundamentally — it transforms knights into bishops overnight! Disruptive technologies not just change the way we live, interact and communicate, but also destroy organisations and entire sectors.

What this essentially means is, attributes that made some organisations ideal for the twentieth century can cripple them in the twenty-first. The existing idea of corporations was built more than hundred and twenty years back. Business management as a subject evolved more than a century ago, in a very nascent era. Therefore, the basic tenets of business need to be rethought and corporations can no longer afford to sit in the sidelines and watch the world go by.

The central objective for earlier businesses was to bring in stability and consolidation. They were built to enforce order. However, in the new era where nothing remains constant, the dominant theme for businesses needs to be speed and imagination. Going forward, companies will be lucky if they can write a five year plan for their business. The future is no longer something that can be painted in black or white. It is a fluid entity that organisations will have to half imagine and half create. Organisations will therefore need to learn how to thrive in chaos.

Finance and accounts departments exist to enforce order into a business. Inevitably, the most powerful people in organisations used to be the accountants. But things have changed since then. Innovation leaders from different disciplines are now coming together and setting the agenda for businesses.

For organisations to survive and succeed in the Creative Economy, innovation has to take centre stage. Soon, the nature of innovation will also change and organisations will have to keep up with that. Macro-innovation, like a new technology, a new product or a new business model will continue to be important. But what will become far more important and decisive is micro-innovation — the ideas and imagination driving day-to-day innovations based on how well a company pre-empts its customers' changing needs and consumption patterns.

The influence of the Creative Economy is already becoming evident across many businesses. In the past, the most successful companies were those that were able to provide either the lowest price or the best quality. Now, in most sectors, price and quality have ceased to be the differentiators. With rigorous processes, outsourcing and quality standards, more than one company in every sector is in a good position to deliver the best quality at the lowest price.

The new macro-differentiator can be design. Design is helping companies to sell differentiated experiences and solutions that connect with the consumer's emotions. It's no longer about selling products and services alone. Nor is it just about completing transactions. Every time a customer walks in, it is an opportunity to build a relationship and invite the customer to become a part of the transformational scenario. Design management is helping us position the customer at the centre of every decision we take and also operate with true entrepreneurial spirit.

It is quite evident that the Creative Economy demands a new way of organisational thinking. Since this change is transformational, business models based on additive changes of the past can no longer be implemented. We need to develop scenario planning tools that will help professionals create favourable scenarios and effect change, rather than react to change.

The organisational structures so far have concentrated on churning out more of the same. Whether it is cars or code, lozenges or legal briefs, the focus has been on hiring similar kind of people who can run assembly lines efficiently. Rigid hierarchies supported by cubicles and cabins are common features of the industrial age corporations. However, none of these environments have been conducive for sustained creativity or innovation.

It is proven fact that diversity leads to creativity. From popular culture to sport, diversity has helped teams perform better. In corporations too, diversity has to be brought in. That is why we have begun to develop cross-functional teams. Having swarms of male management graduates, engineers and accountants isn't good enough. We need more anthropologists, ethnographers, social scientists and most importantly, more women to be part of every team within the organisation.

This revolution has barely begun, and building creative, innovative companies is going to be a huge task. The competition promises to be fierce, and our survival can be at stake if we are not able to adapt to and participate in the changing environment. However, what will be also interesting to see is how corporations collaborate among themselves to generate growth. In the Creative Economy, innovation will also necessarily come through collaboration. And that is evident from some of the most successful innovations that we have seen in recent years — from the Toyota Production System to the way Linux, or more recently Wikipedia, has developed.

It cannot be a zero-sum game anymore. We need to create win-win-win scenarios — where we can win, our business partners can win and the customer can win. Exploiting our bargaining power to get the best terms on each individual contract can kill innovation and long-term collaboration. Instead, the best businesses are being built by leveraging collective strengths and insights that every partner brings on board. 'Innovation networks' or collaborative research and development programs, and 'co-creation' or designing goods and services with collective inputs and insights on consumers, are the new order of the day.

That some of the most respected companies are dramatically transforming their businesses to adapt to the new era is becoming more and more apparent. Apple, from being a designer of world-class consumer products like Mac, has evolved into a designer of consumer experiences like iPOD and iTunes. Technology may be the key driver at Google, but it is so popular because of the simple consumer interface that lies at the core of its design. Management guru Tom Peters, along with other new-age business thinkers, is among the key proponents of many of the ideas mentioned above.

I strongly believe that the future is going to be drastically different from our present and as business organisations, we need to rewrite a lot of established rules. If I am wrong about this world, it will be apparent soon enough. But if I am not wrong, there are a lot of people who will have to go back to school.

The Past	The Future
Stability & Consolidation	Speed & Imagination
Accounting Rules	Innovation Rules
Tangible Assets	Intangible Assets
Delegation	Abdication
TQM, Six Sigma	Design Management
Hierarchy	Seamlessness
Mass Production	Personalisation
Technology Supports Change	Technology Drives Change
Case Studies	Scenario Planning
Products & Services	Experiences & Solutions
PowerPoint Presentations	Storytelling
Enforce Order	Thrive in Chaos
Transaction	Relationships
Competition	Collaboration
Only Men, Engineers, MBAs	More Women, Ethnographers, Designers
Zero Sum Game	Win-Win-Win

Epilogue

A year earlier, Big Bazaar's *Sabse Sasta Din* had generated an unprecedented response from customers. We were able to set a new benchmark in terms of the numbers of customers we attracted and the sales we had generated. However, we had underestimated the power of consumerism in our country. So we were caught off-guard by the huge crowds that gathered outside our stores, waiting to get in.

A year later, we once again announced the Big Bazaar *Sabse Sasta Din* on 26th January 2007. However this time, it wasn't just for a day. We announced that the promotion period will include two more days — the Saturday and Sunday that followed. It was now a three-day event and it generated an even larger response from customers. But this time, we were fully prepared to manage the large number of customers who thronged our stores. We had taken a number of steps to ensure that there were no unruly incidents and customers didn't face any inconveniences.

Interestingly, some of the best insights on crowd management came from temples. Sometime in December, a team from our operations department visited a few of the most popular temples across the country. They picked up lessons on how the large number of devotees, who queue up at temples almost on a daily basis, are managed. Insights on what makes people wait in queues, what they expect, how they behave and what the temple authorities do to control the crowds, were gathered. These were then translated into our context. Basic steps like setting up barricades, making the people move in queues and improving the flow of crowds inside and outside the malls, ensured that the situation never got out of our hands. At many locations we provided water and popcorns to customers who were waiting outside the store. Seating arrangements for senior citizens were also made. Inside the store we increased the number of cash counters and many of our colleagues working at the headquarters or zonal offices extended a helping hand to the store employees.

Much like we were more prepared this time, customers too came in well prepared. One could notice customers wearing sports shoes and carrying water bottles. There were also customers who came in groups. Once they entered the store, each of them headed in different directions within the store, to save time and effort. While some of them shopped, others queued up at the cash counter.

What we realised that day was that if customers see us putting in a lot of effort in helping them, they are willing to forgive a bit of hardship that they may have to go through. The queues were longer this time, but far more organised and orderly. Even though the total number of customers who visited our stores had doubled from last time, at no location did we need to bring additional security or call in the police.

By the end of the three days, more than fifty lakh customers had visited 43 Big Bazaar stores and had spent Rs 125 crore. Indian consumers never fail to surprise us. Once again certain categories and products caught the customers' fancy and sold in unbelievable numbers. Bed sheets for example, were among the highest selling items. If all the bed sheets sold on those three days were stitched together, it could cover the entire city of Amritsar! More than thirty-five thousand mobile handsets were sold, around 1.5 lakh shirts and an equal number of trousers had flown off the shelves. A '555' pack containing five kilos of *atta*, sugar and edible oil each, sold seventy-seven thousand units.

But the story extends way beyond the numbers. Chennai is a city where we haven't been traditionally very strong. We had opened a Pantaloons outlet in Chennai in 2000 and at 26,000 square feet it was the largest store we opened that year. Yet, our success in the city was a limited one and it had taken time to interpret the customers' needs and aspirations in the city. It was only in December 2006 that we opened our first Big Bazaar in Chennai. However, on 26th January 2007 it was the Big Bazaar in Chennai that clocked the highest sales per square feet.

In Kolkata, our first and one of the smallest Big Bazaar stores, is located at V.I.P. Road. Being a small store, it was among the first to shut down last year due to overcrowding. In 2007, the same store did business worth Rs 1 crore on each of the three days.

Another pleasant surprise for us was the popularity of our online initiative that we had launched only a few months back. Internet penetration in India is still at a nascent stage and we had built the business expecting to cater to a very niche segment. But during the *Sabse Sasta Din* promotions at Big Bazaar we decided to offer the same prices and products on the online portal futurebazaar.com. We also set up small booths that had internet connection to this website, as well as catalogues containing pictures and detailed information on the products. A dozen such booths were set up at locations and shopping malls that didn't have a Big Bazaar — for example at Ansal Plaza in New Delhi. Customers could view the offers on the website at the booth or in the catalogues, place the order and we would deliver the products to their homes. It was a small experiment, at a prototype stage and we didn't expect any large business from this initiative.

To our surprise, customers queued up even at these booths. By the end of the three days, the portal had done more business than it had in the preceding month. Some of the customers who ordered through the booths sent post-dated cheques that could be enchased only on the first of next month. It was the end of the month and they didn't have the money to buy. However, they didn't want to miss out on the offers. We gladly accepted such cheques. With this, an online-based retailing model had reached out to customers who may not have ever accessed the internet before.

The *Sabse Sasta Din* event of 26th January, I think, can now be called the marker for when democracy in retail truly set in. For a vast majority of urban Indians the glitzy shopping malls and modern retail formats were perceived to be expensive and exclusive. But on that day, many urban Indians shed their inhibitions for the first time and visited Big Bazaar stores located in shopping malls. And not just Big Bazaar, a lot of other retailers and marketers also joined the fray with various kinds of promotions. It is now a day that truly belongs to every Indian consumer. We are happy that we made it happen in India.